RACIAL FRONTIERS

Racial Frontiers

Africans, Chinese, and Mexicans in Western America, 1848–1890

ARNOLDO DE LEÓN

UNIVERSITY OF NEW MEXICO PRESS

ALBUQUERQUE

To Barry A. Crouch, 1941–2002
Dear Friend and Mentor

LIBRARY OF CONGRESS CATALOGING-IN-PUBLICATION DATA

De León, Arnoldo, 1945–
Racial frontiers : Africans, Chinese, and Mexicans in western America,
1848–1890 / Arnoldo De León.—1st ed.
p.   cm.—(Histories of the American frontier)
Includes bibliographical references and index.
ISBN 0-8263-2271-9 (alk. paper)—ISBN 0-8263-2272-7 (pbk. : alk. paper)
1. West (U.S.)—Ethnic relations.
2. Minorities—West (U.S.)—History—19th century.
3. Minorities—West (U.S.)—Social conditions—19th century.
4. African Americans—West (U.S.)—History—19th century.
5. Chinese Americans—West (U.S.)—History—19th century.
6. Mexican Americans—West (U.S.)—History—19th century.
7. Frontier and pioneer life—West (U.S.)
8. West (U.S.)—History—1848–1860.
9. West (U.S.)—History—1860–1890. I. Title. II. Series.
F596.2 .D4 2002
305.8'00978—dc21
2002002103

DESIGN: MINA YAMASHITA

Contents

Foreword

In American popular culture and much traditional scholarship, the story of America's westward movement is a tale of two races—white men and red skins—that sometimes cooperate but mostly collide. Over the last few decades, however, scholars have brought Africans, Chinese, and Mexicans into the picture. Each of these visible minorities shaped the development of the western frontier and each has had its own historians. In *Racial Frontiers*, Arnoldo De León draws from these discrete historiographies to compare the ways that Africans, Chinese, and Mexicans adapted to an American West dominated by Anglo Americans and their institutions.

Neither Africans, Chinese, nor Mexican immigrants to the West, De León reminds us, represented homogeneous groups of people. Nonetheless, each arrived with a distinctive culture and identity, and each came in search of opportunity. The immigrants' quest sometimes put them in competition with one another. More commonly, however, they competed with Anglo Americans and that, by and large, was a losing game. Whatever their differences, these three groups had the common challenge of navigating the shoals of Anglo American racial prejudice and discrimination. If the West offered opportunities that Africans, Chinese, and Mexicans lacked in their homelands, it did not provide the same opportunities for them that Anglo Americans enjoyed. As it did in the East, the Anglo American majority used a variety of legal, illegal, and extralegal ways to retain control over the key economic, political, and social institutions on the western frontier.

In the face of institutional discrimination, De León tells us, Africans, Chinese, and Mexicans each used the American political system and its courts to fight discrimination and discriminatory legislation. Each group formed mutual aid societies to improve its status. No amount of political or legal initiatives succeeded, however, in lifting these racial minorities beyond second-class citizenship in the Darwinian milieu of the late nineteenth century. With skin that bore the visible marker of their race, Africans, Chinese, and Mexicans could work to counter discrimination but never fully escape it.

Some individuals prevailed to become professionals or to achieve economic success, but Africans, Chinese, and Mexicans found themselves collectively relegated to menial jobs that paid them less than whites for the same work. Their economic circumstances, coupled with their clear racial identity, also hindered their integration into prejudiced Anglo American communities—even in the American West's fluid social environment. As in the East, segregation into racial enclaves kept each group's culture and identity alive long after the frontier era came to an end.

Arnoldo De León's *Racial Frontiers* offers a concise introduction to the history and historiography of Africans, Chinese, and Mexicans on the western frontier, even as it explores the similarities and differences in their experiences. In this fresh, well-told story, De León is as sensitive to the human element as he is to larger patterns. Along with sound generalizations and judicious interpretations he tells the stories of both men and women, many of whom historians had long overlooked.

The C. J. "Red" Davidson Professor of History at Angelo State University in San Angelo, Texas, where he has taught since 1973, Arnoldo De León began this study with an extraordinary understanding of Mexican American history. His earliest works focused on Mexicans in Texas, and a partial list of his books includes *The Tejano Community, 1836–1900* (1982), *They Called them Greasers: Anglo Attitudes toward Mexicans in Texas, 1821–1900* (1983), *Tejanos and the Numbers Game: A Sociohistorical Interpretation from the Federal Censuses, 1850–1900* (1989—co-authored with Kenneth L. Stewart), and *Mexican Americans in Texas: A Brief History* (1993). In the mid-1990s he wrote a book that took him well beyond Texas and reflected one of his broader teaching interests: *North to Aztlán: A History of Mexican Americans in the United States* (1996), co-authored with Richard Griswold del Castillo. Even this broad look at the nation's Mexican American past had not prepared him to write a comparative study of Africans, Chinese, and Mexicans in frontier America. When he bravely accepted our invitation to write this ambitious book, Arnoldo knew he would have to climb a very steep learning curve to understand the experiences of Africans and Chinese immigrants to the West. Climb he did. He has reached a vantage point that gives him and us a view of the American frontier we have not seen before.

Like other books in this series, *Racial Frontiers* tells a complete story, but it is also intended to be read as part of the broader history of western expansion told in these volumes. Each book has been written by a leading authority who brings to the task both a deep knowledge of the subject and well-honed skills of narration and interpretation. Each book provides the general reader with a sound, engaging account of one phase of the nation's frontier past, and offers the specialized student a narrative that is integrated into the general story of the nation's growth.

The distinguished historian Ray Allen Billington conceived the series in 1957 as a narrative history of the American frontier in eighteen volumes. Some of those titles have enjoyed remarkably long lives. Rodman Wilson Paul's *Mining Frontiers of the Far West, 1848–1880,* which first appeared in 1963, was only recently revised by Elliott West (2001). Over the years the series expanded to include topics and geographical units that Ray Billington had not originally envisioned: Sandra L. Myres's *Western Women and the Frontier Experience, 1800–1915* (1982), Elliott West's *Growing Up with the Country: Childhood on the Far Western Frontier* (1989), Donald J. Pisani's *To Reclaim a Divided West: Water, Law, and Public Policy, 1848–1902* (1992), Duane A. Smith, *Rocky Mountain West: Colorado, Wyoming, & Montana, 1859–1915* (1992), Arrell Morgan Gibson and John S. Whitehead's *Yankees in Paradise: The Pacific Basin Frontier* (1993), Terry G. Jordan's multidisciplinary examination of *North American Cattle-Ranching Frontiers: Origins, Diffusion, and Differentiation* (1993), Albert L. Hurtado's *Intimate Frontiers: Sex, Gender, and Culture in Old California* (1999), and James Ronda's *Finding the West: Explorations with Lewis and Clark* (2001). As the series enters its fifth decade, we will continue to explore old frontiers in new ways, as exemplified by Arnoldo De León's *Racial Frontiers.*

—David J. Weber, Southern Methodist University, for the
editors of the *Histories of the American Frontier Series.*

Co-editors:
William Cronon, University of Wisconsin
Howard R. Lamar, Yale University
Martin Ridge, The Huntington Library

Introduction

Mr. Editor:

In every civilized country on the face of the globe, when a soldier is disabled in battle, or by a long term of service, he is liberally rewarded by his government for his services. It is not so in Mexico, where a soldier's term of service is for life and if disabled, he is left in the world to take care of himself the best way he can. If he is fortunate enough to get well, he is again forced into the ranks by press gangs, to-day by one party and to-morrow by another, till his patriotism cools into a captive's feeling, and then seeks his only safety in desertion to the American side. Once on American soil he can breathe the pure air of the true land of liberty....

When the time will come that Mexicans will be allowed to reside in their own country without molestation, then the time will arrive that Mexicans will cease to naturalize themselves into American citizens.... No one has been forced to become naturalized, and those who have done so, have done it voluntarily.... Not all the Mexicans who became naturalized within the last few days, were peons.

No person is allowed to become a citizen of the United States, without being over twenty-one years of age and a resident of the United States for five years. A person twenty-one years of age, and after having resided among Americans for five years, no doubt he knows well what he is about to do, when he holds up his hand and swears in the presence of Almighty God, that he will support the constitution and laws of the United States, and renounced allegiance to all foreign nations, and to the Republic of Mexico particularly.

VARIOUS NATURALIZED MEXICANS

—To the editor of the Brownsville Daily Ranchero, December 4, 1869

This study focuses on racial groups as they met on the trans-Mississippi West. Specifically, it looks at Africans, Chinese, and Mexicans as they crossed paths, competed with each other, and interacted with white Americans and U.S. institutions during the period from circa 1848 to 1890. The book does not give a great deal of space to Anglo Americans, even though they represented a major obstacle to minority opportunity in the West. The Anglo American presence in the drama of the West is used herein essentially for such purposes as comparison and for elucidating more fully the history of racial minorities in the trans-Mississippi setting. Although another racial group—the indigenous Native Americans—was very much a part of the story of the West, they, like Anglo Americans, do not receive much space in this narrative. Other scholars have already answered many of the questions about them posed herein, and the inquisitive student might consult Robert Utley's *The Indian Frontier of the American West, 1846–1890* (Albuquerque: University of New Mexico Press, 1984), one of the most distinguished contributions to the "Histories of the American Frontier" series.

It is a cumbersome task dealing with a subject that involves several different races. True enough, racial minorities may be identified by distinguishable physical marks and by their common fate of facing oppression, exploitation, and segregation to the periphery of society. Whites, of course, have their own distinct physical features and generally belong to the dominant group that determines the fate of the colored minorities. Beyond that, however, problems of identity arise. For instance, Mexicans do not fully conform to the labels of "racial groups" and "peoples of color." Some Mexicans in the West were biologically "white." As was the case in greater Mexico and much of Latin America, however, most were mestizos. Addressing this point, the anthropologist Harold E. Driver once noted that "in Mexico today [1962] more than 80% of the genes in the entire population are probably Indian," with the rest apportioned between the European and African races.[1] Thus, most Mexicans who settled in the American West—the *pobladores*— were a combination of Indians, European Spaniards, and Africans. That being the case, I have taken the liberty of categorizing them as a racially identifiable nonwhite people.

But fitting Mexicans into the category of race is only one problem. None of the racial groups was monolithic: class differences existed among them, for one thing. They disagreed on numerous matters pertinent to their group, among them politics, culture, attitudes toward the United States, and so on. Gender further makes it difficult to treat a group in general terms, for the actions taken by men in making history may not reflect the input and roles of women. Then there is the matter of labels. Within each racial community, members certainly had their own terms of self-ascription, and there were also different "types" within each group. As noted above, a Mexican might be an Indian, a mestizo, or something resembling a European Spaniard. Historians also take liberties in labeling groups, yet those names can change from one generation to another. As a matter of convenience, I have gone with current trends and used "African Americans" or simply "Africans" to identify black Americans; "Chinese" when speaking of those immigrating from China; "Mexicans," "Mexican Americans," or "Hispanic" when I treat Spanish speakers whose origins lay in Mexico; and "whites," "Anglos," or "Anglo Americans" to describe European-descent residents in the West.

Racial Frontiers seeks to meet the need for a book-length multiracial study on people of color who played discernible roles in the settling of the trans-Mississippi West. Certainly it is an effort to fill the void now present in the historiography of the West; often the existing literature either overlooks or is mindless about the contribution of Africans, Chinese, and Mexicans to the frontier experience. Further, the book provides some background, and perhaps some lessons, applicable to a contemporary world where a multitude of races and cultures live in juxtaposition, sometimes harmoniously but sometimes contentiously. The West of the twenty-first century is at once similar to and different from its nineteenth-century predecessor.[2]

In my view, the contact point for Africans, Chinese, Mexicans, and Anglos in the West was a "racial frontier" in that interaction, both incidental and otherwise, involved distinctly identifiable races converging in a specific place. Therein, they sought to live side by side— either in a cooperative or adversarial posture—as well as with the immediate setting.[3] At no time did the engagement embrace an equal

number of these four peoples—white Americans as late as 1890 constituted
90 percent of the population in just about every western state and territory.[4]
Nor did the four interface in every corner of the trans-Mississippi
expanse; encounters occurred in pockets of African, Chinese, and Mexican
settlements. Within these particular areas there were common meeting
places: the town center, ranches, mines, railroad lines, chapels, the parade
field, the gambling table, the brothel, or the marriage bed.

The slave plantations of central Texas served as one specific locale
wherein the destinies of three different frontier groups played themselves
out. There, in the 1850s, Mexicans and blacks joined together, bound by
a common belief and trust in freedom and a common distaste for
Anglo oppression. Mexicans, both natives of the state and other recent
arrivals from Mexico, had established a quasi-underground railroad
designed to facilitate the slaves' escape to Mexico. Defying slave codes
and conventions forbidding fraternizing with the bondspeople,
Mexicans braved both the threatened punishment tied to sabotaging
the peculiar institution and the forbidding terrain on the way to the
Rio Grande to assist runaways. The daring venture brought the expected
condemnation. White citizens from the town of Seguin denounced
Tejanos as "a vagrant class, a lazy, thievish, horde of lazaron [beggar]
who in many instances are fugitives from justice in Mexico, highway
robbers, horse and cattle thieves, and idle vagabonds, who prowl about
our western country with little visible occupations or pursuit." In
other areas of central Texas, those alarmed about slave stealing took a
variety of steps to deal with the Mexican menace: they established
vigilante committees to guard against possible Mexican saboteurs, took
measures to prohibit Mexicans from entering the slave regions, drove
Mexicans out of some of the central Texas counties, or forced unknown
Mexicans into registering upon entering towns.[5]

What came of the different kinds of interracial contacts that entangled
four different races on the frontier? The collusion between pre–Civil
War Mexicans and Africans described above shows that common interests
on the hinterlands could well intertwine the fate of disparate minority
groups. But infinite were the scenarios that could emanate from the
tussling that occurred on the meeting grounds; some of the outcomes

were predictable, most not. At times relations approached the amicable. Competitors might pursue accommodation with their rivals, but the mood between peoples more likely was confrontational. Between 1848 and 1890, race relations generally dictated a balancing act between hostile competition and coexistence as all involved maneuvered for position and advantage in a setting deemed a place of new beginnings.

In trying to explain what happens "when cultures meet," I posit the frontier to be a lightly settled region where people arrive with high expectations for uplifting themselves. The players compete in the physical/social environment, jockeying for a political/economic/social niche in that "place." The contest produces changes among all those involved as the subjects make concessions to the setting and to institutions that regulate the cadence of political and economic life. Simultaneously, however, the groups resist the transforming power of the frontier and retain aspects of their social framework and elements of their homeland culture.⁶

To Africans, Chinese, and Mexicans, therefore, the frontier was a psychological construct, just as it was for anyone else who entered it. For minorities, the trans-Mississippi expanse represented a geographic area that offered the possibility of starting anew, or of achieving material rewards through hard work and resolve. The frontier afforded them refuge, or an escape to freedom. There, also, a pioneer might attain success without obligation to forego old social and cultural tenets. Anglo Americans—the traditional subjects associated with the settlement of the Far West—held not too different visions of the same setting. As a long line of historians has argued, the frontier for white Americans might not have been a heaven on earth, but it represented the possibility for improvement over place of origin. Opportunities made available in a developing region offered hope of material acquisition and social progression, if not for the first generation, then for children or grandchildren. Any headway was to take place within the context of a familiar cultural milieu.⁷

Such was the case with the "Exodusters" who immigrated willy-nilly to Kansas in 1879. They were not the first blacks to have been lured by myths of Kansas as a land of renewal and advancement: real estate promoters in years previous had settled several hundred former slaves and their descendants in the state. But intolerable conditions in the postwar South forced the poorest of African Americans to take a chance on an El Dorado. Though most had neither the resources nor the frontier experience to risk the venture, the lure of Kansas came to be irresistible by the latter years of the 1870s. Fast-talking rascals and sundry opportunists masquerading as land impresarios wanting to help an oppressed people relocate to the West lay behind the new excitement. Frauds looking for the Africans' last buck distributed literature throughout various parts of the South that publicized fertile lands to be parceled out in Kansas by the national government. Posters, circulars, and photos found their way south describing Kansas as prejudice-free. Illustrations depicted a life of ease and prosperity for black settlers in Kansas. Stories ostensibly emanating from Kansas by black immigrants described the state as extending unrivaled hospitality to those choosing it as their destination.[8]

Many made up their minds that Kansas was the place to be. In the excitement, Kansas was transformed into a setting where opportunity offered itself to anyone regardless of skin color or ancestry and where an honest day's toil rendered tangible results. From what people understood, the federal government would provide free transportation westward. For nominal fees paid to "agents," settlers expected to receive free land, farm implements, and start-up capital. Supplies might be acquired on credit. Prospective pioneers envisioned themselves building modest but comfortable homes in a land where wild game was plentiful enough to meet dietary needs.[9] Some seven thousand "believers" imbued with Kansas fever headed west in 1879 as a result of the fervor created by the profit seekers, though many others were responding to calls by earlier black colonizers who settled in Kansas. Disorganized and unfamiliar with the new lands, and lacking homes and food, the newcomers believed their exodus (thus the term "Exodusters") would take them to the "Promised Land." Instead, they barely survived the cold weather. The migration ended within the year, but a few of the Exodusters did remain in Kansas as permanent settlers.[10]

In entering the trans-Mississippi West, the Exodusters had understood that fulfilling their expectations would call for sacrifice, starting from scratch, and surviving perils. Like other westering folks, African Americans surely understood that in pursuit of their aspirations they would contend with exploitation, racism, discouragement, and perhaps failure. But they expected that tenacity in the face of adversity might well lead to an improved status for all concerned. Such a frontier "ideal" survives today in the minds of noncitizens who enter industrial urban settings: many willingly work as custodians, roofers, kitchen helpers, construction workers, and at other physically exhausting labor so their offspring will benefit from the American promise.

It is, of course, a well-known principle that race handicaps such aspirations, whether in the nineteenth century or today. In the 1850s through the 1880s, racial minorities (unlike their white neighbors) pursued life ambitions in the West burdened by skin color and physiognomy. The Exodusters, their dreams notwithstanding, would not have found equality in the Sunflower State no matter how much they accepted the ways of whites, adapted to mainstream institutions, or jettisoned homeland customs. Race has a way of deterring people of color from sharing in the fruits that the dominant white society generally takes for granted.

This volume on the trans-Mississippi West excludes the slave states of Missouri, Arkansas, Louisiana, and eastern Texas (that region of the state with close ties to the Deep South). Throughout the text, the term "trans-Mississippi West" means all states and territories west of the Mississippi River except these former slave states (and Texas loosely east of the 98th meridian). The book covers a forty-year span. It begins about the time of the American-Mexican War when Oregon and Washington became U.S. territories, Mexico's Far North was absorbed into the United States, and people of many nationalities and races rushed into California for gold. It ends with 1890, the concluding date for many of the volumes in the "Histories of the American Frontier" series. This cutoff year eliminates other major Asian groups—Japanese, Filipinos, Koreans, and Vietnamese among them—from the study, for the period of these people's migration to the United States occurred in the late nineteenth or twentieth centuries.

Much responsible for the final product is David J. Weber, who solicited the work some years back for the "Histories of the American Frontier" series. From the start, he assured me of any good historian's ability to master a subject area outside her/his specialty; he then guided and encouraged me along the way. Of great value in bringing together my ideas on the racial frontier was a most constructive critique of an early draft by Durwood Ball. Dr. Ball, then a member of the University of New Mexico Press's editorial staff, succinctly explained to me the manner by which I could interweave different racial experiences into a sensible, interesting, and provocative narrative. David Holtby remained as cordial and supportive of the book as he has of my other works that the University of New Mexico Press has published since 1982. Gratitude also goes to the late Barry A. Crouch of Gallaudet University in Washington, D.C., and to my colleague Guoqiang Zheng of Angelo State University. Both read the entire work and offered helpful commentary on all chapters.

CHAPTER 1

Push-Pull

Leaving the Troubled Homeland

I know not whether I will better my condition by going, but I am determined never to surrender to adversity, until the last hope has withered. I have fought him [adversity] long and hard—often he has had the best of the conflicts. I have never declined yet to give him battle when attacked by him.

—Douglas Henry Daniels,
PIONEER URBANITES: A SOCIAL AND CULTURAL
HISTORY OF BLACK SAN FRANCISCO

The author of such forceful words was a black miner, not pondering an omen but affirming how life's travails only strengthened his will. He wrote from Silver City, Idaho, in 1869 just as he, like most everyone else in the region, parted for another spot in the West, seeking their destiny at the next mother lode. His audience was the readership of the San Francisco *Examiner,* who might take to heart the indomitable courage of fellow African Americans like himself who saw the mines (or the frontier for that matter) as springboards for material betterment. Indeed, his resolve mirrored that of other peoples of color in the West, fully prepared to face formidable odds in order to achieve set goals and reach high expectations. Most came to the trans-Mississippi region conditioned to sacrifice, compete, and face hardship head-on, believing opportunity in the West to be unquestionably more appealing than the despair plaguing the homeland.

On January 24, 1848, James W. Marshall, in the act of constructing a sawmill at John Sutter's ranch in the valley of the Sacramento River, discovered gold. The resulting rush to California raised the specter of instant wealth for persons of every stripe, and in practically no time ambition had thrown together people of every race, many of whom had never encountered folks quite so different from themselves. African Americans, Asians, and Mexicans navigated their way into this racial frontier, harboring the same optimism for quick fortunes as white Americans and Europeans, the group generally associated with this monumental drama in Western history.

News of the California strike spread to China via sea captains who advertised that wealth could be amassed in quick time. They aimed to drum up fresh business in the form of paid passengers; in fact, many anchored at Hong Kong harbor to acquire a shipload of Chinese emigrants and sail them into the expected Promised Land. By the early 1850s, some of the early arrivals had either sent news of their good fortune back home to their families, or returned to their birthplace with stories confirming the potential for riches in what they called the Gold Mountain.[1]

Chinese who came to the trans-Mississippi West between 1848 and 1882 (on the latter date, Congress passed the Chinese Exclusion Act) hailed from the coastal province of Kwangtung (also spelled Guangdong) in the southeastern part of China. Geographically, Kwangtung was isolated from the rest of China by a mountain mass in the north. Canton (also spelled Guangzhou) is the provincial capital of Kwangtung; it is located just north of the Pearl River Delta, a fertile basin situated where the Pearl River (and its tributaries) flow into the South China Sea. The Pearl River Delta served as the economic center of the Kwangtung Province.[2]

Most historians have explained that Kwangtung sent more Chinese to the United States than any other province because its people wished to escape distress brought on by the declining Ch'ing (Qing) dynasty (1644–1911). Additionally, people suffered economically due to China's loss in the Opium War (1839–1842), following which Great Britain forced large indemnities on the country and supplanted Chinese merchants in Canton. As England flooded the Chinese market with its imports, domestic textile and handicraft industries reeled, displacing thousands of people from supportive occupations in Kwangtung.[3] Other factors exacerbated the people's dilemma. Wealthy landlords in Kwangtung continued the push toward amassing new farm acreage, absorbing small plots in the process. So many souls lived in the Kwangtung province by the mid-nineteenth century that its lands could not grow enough foodstuffs to sustain them.⁴ Simultaneously, the people of the Pearl River Delta experienced a series of natural calamities that stifled farming and produced starvation: a major drought in 1851, a terrible flood the next year, then a new onslaught of drought and heavy rains in parts of Kwangtung province in 1854. As if the above were not enough, fighting broke out throughout the nation during the 1850s and 1860s in the form of popular rebellions against the government and in civil wars engaging competing clans. The ruinous political and economic conditions that plagued Kwangtung at mid-century did not abate throughout the 1860s and 1870s.⁵

One historian, however, downplays this gloomy explanation for emigration to the U.S. West. The Opium War, he argues, did not devastate Canton as a center of international trade; the city remained prosperous long into the twentieth century. While the Opium War harmed the textile industry in Kwangtung province, people found alternative kinds of work, either in the rural sector or in the region's market economy. Other conditions described by an earlier generation of scholars also appear overdrawn. Land dispossession occurred, but it afflicted the poor long before the mid-nineteenth century; demographic growth existed, but it was long-standing and the province could feed itself by either importing goods or selling a variety of crops for profit; climatic convulsion certainly took its toll on the villages, yet such a phenomenon was not all that calamitous; famine plagued many, but it was never extreme; rebellions were a part of mid-century turmoil, but they affected other parts of the country from where people did not emigrate; and while civil war erupted, some of the fighting did not actually take place in Kwangtung province—in fact, part of it occurred following the initial wave of migration to the United States during the early 1850s.

This new interpretation asserts that, for the most part, the Pearl River Delta during the 1850s through the 1880s was economically sound and culturally prosperous. It remained, in the view of this revisionist, a fertile agricultural region producing oranges, tobacco, and other sundry crops for sale in outside markets and a center of international trade. The work force included a mix of merchants, artisans, and day laborers; the latter traveled throughout the province in search of jobs. Canton throughout the century retained its standing as the main port of export and entry for various goods and supplies. It maintained ties with numerous contact points in the Pacific, including California.

Just as the Pearl River area continued as a successful economic region in China, so was it a thriving cultural mecca. It was consistently exposed, via Canton, to news from beyond China, and it offered as much cultural richness to outsiders as it absorbed. This connection to the rest of the world, including California, permitted the people of Kwangtung to learn about the gold rush in the early 1850s. According to this recent point of view, those who left for the U.S. West in the 1850s through 1882 were not famished, backward, and demoralized beings tragically vulnerable to the harshness of the Western frontier. Certainly some impoverished Chinese left for California and the West, but with them went others with the means and temperament to make the journey. They brought to the United States their experience as versatile day laborers, skilled craftsmen, merchants, and the like. Most Chinese pioneers made a calculated judgment to emigrate, and they arrived on the frontier with a "vision" of the sacrifice and effort required for success in the U.S. West.[6] This general portrayal of Chinese emigrant background jibes with a widely accepted premise regarding Anglo American migration into the Far West: that relocating from the East to the trans-Mississippi region was an undertaking many times prohibitive to the poorest folks.[7]

The prospect of unbound possibilities in California motivated many a young man from the Pearl River Delta to sail east toward the United States. The opportunity for a new start was made easier following mutual agreement on the Burlingame Treaty of 1868, in which the Chinese government legally recognized emigration into the United States. In negotiating it, the United States had as one of its intentions the importation of cheap laborers who would assist in the laying of railroad lines throughout the trans-Mississippi West.[8] Whether before or after 1868, villagers visualized finding employment in the United States, working for a few years, then returning to China with money saved. To finance their trip, the emigrants relied on a variety of methods, but the credit ticket system (which lasted from circa 1852 to 1882, the year when Congress stopped further Chinese immigration) became the common plan. Under this arrangement, a person received a credit ticket from a local entrepreneur in Kwangtung and then pledged to work until the lender had been reimbursed with interest (usually an obligation erased within a few months after the emigrant's arrival). The agreement was, therefore, not a form of contract servitude wherein persons committed themselves to working off the expense of their passage over a designated time. To the contrary, the accord implied that the subjects involved were at liberty to go their own way upon repaying their debt. Most Chinese immigrants entered the system voluntarily and accepted it as a practical way to get to the United States. As such, they were not "coolies"—a term connoting slavery or peonage—and historians have taken pains to correct this misconception about the status of nineteenth century Chinese immigrants.[9]

Points of departure were the ports of Hong Kong and Canton. The voyage stretched over a distance of some seven thousand miles and consumed much time. The early vessels that brought emigrants to San Francisco during the 1850s and 1860s required anywhere from two to three months—comparatively, the overland journey from the eastern United States to California required three to six months. After steamships became an alternative means of travel by the later 1860s, Chinese emigrants could expect about a one-month journey to Gold Mountain.[10]

Once on the ship, passengers faced a horrendous crossing, for skippers generally overloaded their vessels to maximize profits. Designed for carrying cargo and not people, the sailing vessels lacked adequate facilities. The passengers suffered from poor ventilation, improper diets, and little protection from the weather, factors that made them vulnerable to disease. Some fell victim to violence, as fighting erupted between rivals from back home. Deaths from conditions on board were not uncommon; indeed, sources estimate that 10 percent of the human cargo was lost on some voyages.[11]

Upon arriving at the west coast, usually San Francisco, Chinese emigrants were met by fellow countrymen—friends, relatives, or contractors, the latter generally from one of several associations born in

California during the 1850s that gradually evolved into the Chinese Six Companies (which represented the six districts in China from which most of the Chinese in San Francisco originated). Those receiving the new arrivals then led the immigrants to the Chinese quarter, where acquaintances helped them find employment or where the associations assigned them to work in the mines, railroads, or other types of occupations.[12]

Among the first Chinese to have seen Gold Mountain was Maria Seise, who arrived aboard ship in San Francisco in 1848 as a servant girl. Maria's passage to California had been less dreadful than that experienced by most male immigrants, yet her past was no less turbulent. She had fled from Canton as a young girl to escape the real possibility of being sold into bondage by her destitute parents. Foreigners in China always needed servant help, and fortune had allowed her to find such work on a consistent basis. While under the employ of a Portuguese family, she had converted to Catholicism. Her work as a family domestic took her to Hawaii and then back to China, where in 1843 she serendipitously landed a job with the family of a New York trader named Charles V. Gillespie. In the year before the gold rush, Maria Seise left Hong Kong with the Gillespies and two other Chinese men who also accompanied the family.[13]

The two men who arrived with Maria Seise soon departed for the gold fields, and though it is believed that Maria remained with the Gillespies, little is known of her life as it unfolded in the West. Much the same thing happened to subsequent immigrants from China. They became anonymous figures who dispersed throughout the frontier to lead ordinary lives, yet who constituted the foundation for Chinese American communities.

Most of the Chinese during the nineteenth century made California home, with much of the population concentrated in San Francisco.[14] But dispersal after the 1850s also occurred into various sections of the trans-Mississippi region, particularly toward the Northwest and the Rocky Mountain states of Montana, Idaho, and Nevada.[15] According to one historian, 90 percent of Chinese settlers in the United States in 1890 lived in West Coast states, mainly California.[16]

Maria Seise entered the racial frontier long after ethnic or racial Mexicans—mestizos—had made parts of the U.S. West their place of residence. A mestizo population had accompanied pobladores (settlers) such as Rosa María Hinojosa de Ballí into the southernmost sections of modern-day Texas since New Spain's colonial era. While Rosa María (1752–1803) came from a different social and economic station than did Maria Seise, her migration north within the Spanish empire was equally fraught with uncertainty. Though born into privilege—she was the daughter of a prominent Spanish official in government service and she received a private education—she had lived a frontier experience as part of Spain's efforts to occupy its far northern regions. Her family had come to Tamaulipas as part of a colonization venture led by José de Escandón, and she then married José María Ballí, an officer in the royal military. Her marriage to Ballí solidified her status as a member of the upper crust in the local social hierarchy around Reynosa, but tragedy struck when her husband died, leaving her widowed with three sons and a land grant of several leagues in what today is the Lone Star State.

Doña Rosa remained in Reynosa but, making the most of Spanish society's tolerance for women who engaged in business ventures, she expanded her initial inheritance in the north by buying thousands of acres along the Rio Grande Valley in today's counties of Hidalgo, Cameron, Willacy, Starr, and Kenedy. Periodically she crossed the Rio Grande to oversee her Texas properties, which she stocked with herds of horses and cattle. Success earned her the title of the first "Cattle Queen of Texas."[17]

Into Doña Rosa's estates went ranch hands and settlers representing the initial ranks of Spanish/Mexican pobladores who then dispersed throughout the Borderlands and encountered Anglos and other peoples of color when they arrived in the Far North following the war with Mexico. But by no means were these early pioneers the last to enter the region. The new mining strikes throughout the U.S. Southwest pulled thousands of men from Mexico; the flood of miners into California in 1849 and the early 1850s was followed by other excursions into the mines of Nevada, Arizona, and Colorado.

Other aspects of the developing economy in the West after 1848 similarly lured migrants. Villagers who had traditionally pursued seasonal employment in Mexico now shuttled back and forth from their native land into parts of the trans-Mississippi West; after a period many stayed permanently. Underemployed ranch and farm peons from Mexico's north, *arrieros* (freighters), miners, and artisans who were determined to change sovereignties received improved pay in the West's lumber industry, the railroads, land reclamation projects, mines, and ranches and farms.[18]

For members of the better classes in Mexico, the U.S. West offered an alternative to life under Mexico's dictatorship and possibilities for a new prosperity, perhaps through investments in business, commerce, or landholding. Then too, stories of the mythic West filtered back. That lore seduced those adventuresome spirits in Mexico wanting to explore unknown lands. Accompanying the above "pull" forces were "push" forces: humankind's instinct for survival, the desire to improve the self, and the need to care for loved ones pushed impoverished folks to try to ameliorate their poverty elsewhere.

Those coming from the Mexican states of Sonora, Zacatecas, Chihuahua, Sinaloa, and Durango struck for California, energizing Hispanic settlements that traced their beginnings to the last three decades of the eighteenth century. Discontented residents of Sonora, meanwhile, headed into Arizona, as immigrants from Nuevo León, Tamaulipas, and Coahuila augmented the Texas Mexican population.[19] Less immigration from Mexico occurred into New Mexico and Colorado, though each retained a Hispanic presence throughout the nineteenth century.[20]

Biddy Mason traveled West as property, owned by Robert Marion Smith and his wife, a slave-holding family from Mississippi. The Smiths had converted to Mormonism in the 1840s, and in 1848 packed their belongings (including several slaves), joined an expedition in Fulton, Missouri, and headed for Utah to assist the augmentation of the Mormon kingdom. Terrible problems, including alternating conditions of rain and drought, stalked the caravan as it traveled by wagon and riverboat. The trip imposed incredible demands upon Biddy Mason.

Besides caring for the Smith youngsters, performing the usual slave chores, and minding her own small children, who included an infant, she had to guard the family's cattle and take on any new task that might surface unexpectedly. In Mississippi, she had acquired knowledge in midwifery, and it is believed that she either assisted in or personally helped deliver some of the babies born to women on the trail west. After arriving in Salt Lake City, the Smiths and their slaves settled down in their new homes for some three years, but then picked up once more, this time joining a caravan of 150 wagons destined for San Bernardino, California. The group sought to found a new settlement that would act as a resting stop for other Mormons going to Utah by sailing around South America.[21]

The black dispersal into the West was not so much along the west coast, as with the Chinese and perhaps even the Mexicans. In 1890, most African Americans in the trans-Mississippi West were to be found in Kansas and Oklahoma, followed by California, Iowa, Nebraska, and Minnesota, although Colorado featured a sizable population due to an influx of black miners drawn to its gold rush of the late 1850s. Other areas of the West contained black settlements, but these were not as visible as those in the Plains region and California."[22] Nonetheless, black population pockets toward the end of the century were to be found in unlikely spots—among them the Pacific Slope along the British/U.S. border, where one George Washington Bush had joined the pioneering march to the Northwest. Born in the northern United States, he had received schooling in Philadelphia, for he came from a family of modest standing (his parents had inherited money from their white master). During the 1830s he experimented with farming in Missouri and, though successful, relocated to the Oregon country in 1844, in part because he along with others in the United States caught "Oregon Fever," but also to escape the racial prejudice that visited his five sons, whose mother incidentally was of German-American heritage.

Like so many of his westering contemporaries, Bush was not a novice at frontier living. Before settling down and starting a family, he had been a fur trader in the West, and indeed had traversed different parts of the trans-Mississippi on several occasions. Despite his race, he had apparently been able to cope with the social environment in Missouri, having prospered in farming and earning the respect and confidence of fellow white yeomen. But as with many others settlers out West, he also clung to the chance that a potential El Dorado lay just over the next horizon.

In moving to Oregon he had not escaped prejudice. Too many racists from Missouri had arrived there in the frenzy of the moment, and they preemptively passed ordinances prohibiting "free Negroes" from inhabiting the territory. Along with other white settlers who had accompanied him to the Oregon country, Bush in 1845 headed north past the Columbia River into a land presumably beyond the jurisdiction of the Oregon laws, for the British claimed that section of the continent. When the United States acquired that portion of the Northwest from the British in 1846, however, "free Negroes" were banned from residence there.

Bush had been a frontiersman too long to be deterred from finding a niche in the West. His generosity, goodwill, and neighborliness toward others during frontier crises in Missouri, on the trek west, and in Oregon proper had earned him trusted friends and followers who prevailed upon the territorial government to have him exempt from the legislation excluding folks of his race from Oregon. Though permitted by legislators to stay in Oregon, he could not own property, vote, use the courts, or exercise rights granted to whites. Despite such disadvantages, he continued working his farm in Puget Sound, and with true pioneer altruism shared with neighbors the bountifulness of his land and the wealth he had inherited before heading toward the Northwest. In 1854, friends in what was then the Washington Territory petitioned Congress to allow Bush ownership of his farmlands, a concession Congress made the next year. By a combination of forethought, tenacity, perseverance, instinct for survival, and prowess in the face of overwhelming hurdles, Bush had struck a bonanza in the northwestern frontier, even as his status remained that of a second-class citizen. He died in 1863, but his sons made sure the old farmstead thrived.[23]

How many people of color actually made their way west from 1848 to 1890? Compared to white Americans and Europeans, not many: the U.S. census of population was always nebulous on the matter. It put the figure for African Americans at about 1,500 in 1850 and at approximately

Table 1. Racial Populations in the Trans-Mississippi West, 1850–90

STATE	AFRICAN AMERICANS					CHINESE AMERICANS					ANGLO-AMERICANS[a]				
	1850	1860	1870	1880	1890	1850	1860	1870	1880	1890	1850	1860	1870	1880	1890
Arizona	—	—	26	155	1,357	—	—	20	1,630	1,170	—	—	9,581	35,160	55,580
California	962	4,086	4,272	6,018	11,322	—	34,933	49,277	75,132	72,472	92,635	323,177	499,424	767,181	1,111,672
Colorado	—	46	456	2,435	6,215	—	—	7	612	1,398	—	34,231	39,221	191,126	404,468
Idaho	—	—	60	53	201	—	—	4,274	3,379	2,007	—	—	10,618	29,013	82,013
Iowa	333	1,069	5,762	9,516	10,685	—	—	3	3	64	192,881	673,779	1,188,207	1,614,600	1,901,086
Kansas	—	627	17,018	43,107	49,710	—	—	—	19	93	—	166,390	346,377	952,155	1,376,533
Minnesota	39	259	759	1,564	3,683	—	—	—	24	94	6,038	169,395	438,257	776,884	1,296,159
Montana	—	—	183	346	1,490	—	—	1,949	1,765	2,532	—	—	18,306	35,385	127,271
Nebraska	—	82	789	2,385	8,913	—	—	—	18	214	—	28,696	122,117	449,764	1,046,888
Nevada	—	45	357	488	242	—	—	3,152	5,416	2,833	—	6,812	38,959	53,556	39,084
New Mexico	22	85	172	1,015	1,996	—	—	—	57	361	61,525	89,924	90,393	108,721	142,719
North Dakota	—	—	94	401	373	—	—	—	238	28	—	2,576	12,887	133,147	182,123
Oklahoma	—	[b]	—	—	2,973	—	—	—	—	25	—	—	—	—	58,826
Oregon	207	128	346	487	1,186	—	—	3,330	9,510	9,540	13,087	52,160	86,929	163,075	301,758
Dakota Terr.	—	—	—	—	541	—	—	—	—	195	—	—	—	—	327,290
Texas[d]	—	—	5,742	9,921	12,006	—	—	—	2	398	—	—	66,253	224,380	409,950
Utah	59	59	118	232	588	—	—	445	501	806	11,330	40,125	86,044	142,423	205,899
Washington	—	30	207	325	1,602	—	—	234	3,186	3,260	—	11,138	22,195	67,199	340,513
Wyoming	—	—	183	298	922	—	—	143	914	465	—	—	8,726	19,437	59,275

Source: *Report on Population of the United States at the Eleventh Census: 1890.* Part I, "General Tables" (Washington, D.C.: Government Printing Office, 1895), pp. 400–401.

a Includes the Mexican American population.

b Quintard Taylor, *In Search of the Racial Frontier: African Americans in the American West, 1528–1990* (New York: W. W. Norton Company, 1998), p. 69, puts the slave population in 1860 at 7,367.

c W. Sherman Savage, *Blacks in the West* (Westport, Conn.: Greenwood Press, 1976), appendix, places the number at 21,000.

d West of the 98th meridian. Source: *Report on Population of the United States at the Eleventh Census: 1890,* Part I, "General Tables," table 15: "Native and Foreign Born and White and Negro Population by Counties: 1870–1890," pp. 430–33; table 16: "Chinese Population by Counties: 1870–1890," pp. 440–41.

130,000 as of 1890 (see table 1).[24] What explains the matter of slow black westward migration during the nineteenth century? Historians dismiss distance and poverty, for thousands of white Americans took the risk of the overland journey in an attempt at a new life in the West. Racism might have acted as a deterrent, but it prevailed in the industrial North as well. Desolation, tribulation, and remoteness from black communities certainly discouraged relocation, but such obstacles existed for whites as well. A haunting conviction that the West offered black settlers no better economic opportunity than other parts of the country seems to be a more persuasive force behind the modest figures, scholars believe. In the West, many white workers competed for the best jobs in a developing economy, emerging labor unions jealously guarded employment opportunities, and, unfortunately for blacks, railroad and mining companies preferred Chinese or Mexican labor.[25]

While the 1850 decennial census officially reported 74,302 Spanish-surnamed people living in the U.S. Southwest as of mid-century, scholars have questioned that figure since census takers during the frontier age were prone to miss transients, settlers in remote areas, or others wishing to avoid detection by officials. Modern researchers, taking into account a variety of factors in their calculations, have offered new counts for the total U.S. Hispanic population at mid-century. One lower estimate places the number of Mexican-descent settlers living in the United States in 1850 at somewhere between 80,000 and 90,000. A higher estimate offered by Oscar J. Martínez puts the number living in the United States at between 87,000 and 118,000.[26]

Determining the number of Mexican-descent settlers for the year 1890 is even more difficult because the original manuscript census has perished (thereby preventing a hand count). Nonetheless, imaginative calculations provide some idea of its total. Relying upon base figures for 1850, adding the immigrant population provided in the censuses for every decade, and allowing for probable annual growth, Martínez notes that between 290,000 and 423,000 Mexican-origin people resided in the United States during the year 1890.[27]

The number of Chinese immigrants grew steadily during the period 1848 to 1890, though it always remained rather small compared

Table 2. Percent of Total Population in 1890 by Race

State	African Americans	Chinese Americans	Anglo-Americans[a]
Arizona	2.28	2.02	93.22
California	0.94	6.01	92.02
Colorado	1.51	0.37	98.12
Idaho	0.24	2.40	97.19
Iowa	0.56	0.01	99.43
Kansas	3.48	0.01	96.46
Montana	1.13	1.96	96.30
Nebraska	0.84	0.03	98.86
Nevada	0.53	6.13	85.41
New Mexico	1.27	0.26	92.02
North Dakota	0.20	0.02	99.67
Oklahoma	4.81	0.07	95.14
Oregon	0.38	3.04	96.17
South Dakota	0.16	0.07	99.54
Texas[b]	2.92	0.001	97.08
Utah	0.28	0.40	99.04
Washington	0.46	1.06	97.46
Wyoming	1.52	0.81	97.64

Source: *Report on Population of the United States at the Eleventh Census: 1890,* Part I
(Washington, D.C: Government Printing Office, 1895), p. c1.

a Includes the Mexican American population.
b West of the 98th meridian. Source: *Report on Population of the United States at the Eleventh Census: 1890,* Part I, "General Tables," table 15: "Native and Foreign Born and White and Negro Population by Counties: 1870–1890," pp. 430–32; table 16: "Chinese Population by Counties: 1870–1890," pp. 440–41.

to the Mexican-descent population. At least two things might explain the low figures. A strong sense of ethnocentrism discouraged Chinese people from leaving the homeland—traditionally the Chinese had considered other civilizations inferior. Then, until the 1860s, there existed the penalty of death by decapitation, a policy long followed by the Ch'ing government to discourage political opponents from fleeing the country and plotting the dynasty's overthrow from abroad (for example, from Taiwan).[28]

In 1850, slightly over 4,000 Chinese people lived in the United States. After the government in China eased its restrictions on immigration during the 1860s (restrictions that China formally repudiated in the Burlingame Treaty of 1868) and the United States publicized its need for cheap laborers to work in the trans-Mississippi West, the number of those arriving in the United States climbed: about 64,000 Chinese people came during the 1860s and another 123,000 in the decade of the 1870s. At the time Congress stopped Chinese immigration in 1882, some 132,000 persons of Chinese descent lived in the United States, and the federal census put their number at 107,488 in 1890. About 91 percent of these lived in the trans-Mississippi West (table 2).[29]

Most certainly the people who settled the West differed in discernible ways. They came from distinguishable regions of North America as well as from distant continents. They arrived by different routes and modes of travel. Some found themselves in settings that represented a radical departure from the milieu they left behind. Others settled in very familiar environments. How different, for example, were the Chinese from the Mexicans? The former came from a faraway world and survived the perilous waters of the Pacific Ocean, while the latter crossed an artificial boundary over familiar terrain. African Americans—as in the example of George Washington Bush—had the least cultural adjustment to make, while most Mexicans and practically all Chinese spoke no English and lacked an immediate understanding of the social environment before them. On the other hand, Mexicans often settled in regions of the West where stable Hispanic communities were of long standing. That experience was not common for Africans, and certainly not the case for the Chinese, who had to establish communities de novo.

But despite differences, all who headed into the trans-Mississippi West reached their destination fit and ready to confront whatever exigencies existed in the region. Spanish/Mexican pioneers, for one, derived from stock hardened by generations of endurance on the frontier; particularly adept and equipped for survival under the most difficult conditions were the legendary *norteños,* those pobladores from states in Mexico's northern periphery. As a group, the norteños had achieved a reputation for resilience in the face of isolation. In the hinterlands they wrestled with the indigenous tribes, solitude, and nature itself, yet succeeded in sinking roots and implanting Spain's, and later Mexico's, political and social institutions. Without a ready supply of Indian labor at hand (as was the case in the central regions of New Spain), they relied consistently upon their own energies to turn the lands of the Far North into life-sustaining resources. They developed appropriate methods to work the farmlands and honed work skills to manage their livestock; a certain ethic among them recognized the equality of vaqueros out on the range. Lacking frontier protection from the central government, civilians molded essential fighting skills to battle the *indios bárbaros;* soldiers who led the defense of the region often would retire in the Far North and add their own experience in Indian fighting to the local communities. Their tradition of challenging the fiercest tribes (among them the Yaqui, the Pima, and the Mayo) earned the norteños a reputation for daring and macho gallantry.[30]

People who struck from their homelands for the trans-Mississippi West—whether Africans, Chinese, or Mexicans—thus arrived seasoned to grapple with the physical environment they encountered. The vast majority of immigrants were already hardy veterans of rugged lives, having led a rather hardscrabble existence. Most came from circumstances that offered few conveniences. In the rural environs they called home, life revolved around grinding poverty. Such a misfortune meant having to earn a livelihood by relying on the ax and the plow, hauling potable water, and fetching wood from some distances. As a fact of life they endured the seasons, suffering through heat and insects or, at the other extreme, cold weather and winter hunger. Most made do without the proper household items (including comfortable sleeping accommodations), put up with unsanitary conditions (outside privies, floorless huts or cabins, and no baths), survived despite inadequate diets, and did their best to dress themselves appropriately given scarce supplies. Additionally, they combated disease, infant mortality, and accidents that occurred in the workplace. Immigrants were rugged individuals—already "toughened up" by their own frontier long before they penetrated the backcountry that was the U.S. West. Most were tested "survivalists," heirs to experiences that had stared down man, nature, and mishap throughout the ages.

Wrestling with the frontier's social environment was a matter different from adapting to the terrain of the hinterlands. Fending off nature's perils and its landscape was one thing, but pioneer people of color lacked experience interfacing with other racial groups and with local tribes challenging them (generally unsuccessfully) for provincial domination. Within living memory Chinese and Mexicans had not dealt with peoples other than of their own color, background, and tradition. In contrast to whites, who entered and implanted a familiar social environment, people of color knew little of the language, customs, and institutions endemic to the post-1848 West. Only Africans had prior familiarity with the social ambiance constituting the trans-Mississippi West, and thus had the least cultural adaptation to make. But even they entered the region disadvantaged, as slaves or former slaves who had to make a radical adjustment to freedom.

Further hampering habituation to the social environment in the West was the fact that Africans, Chinese, and Mexicans did not descend from social classes cocksure of themselves. In their respective places of origin, violence and oppression directed at the working poor were a fact of life, as were intimidation, indifference to their poverty, and a disregard for their existence. Subordination to an upper class meant having to withstand abuse, exploitation, and disdain for their social rank, while simultaneously carrying out psychological resistance against the oppressor. Such a state of affairs most certainly begot a sense of fraternity and camaraderie that revolved around the common experiences each community shared (*la raza* in the case of Mexicans). Despite such group solidarity and cohesiveness, most arrived cautiously, warily, timidly, and with practically no background in the art of confidently asserting themselves before those better able to enforce and protect vested interests.

Frontier people of color preferred retaining imported customs and traditions even when strategy dictated that they forego links to the homeland identity. The newcomers chose fidelity to the past, in part because of an inherent suspicion they had developed toward despotic societies. Over the decades of the nineteenth century, for instance, the people of Mexico had fought Native American tribes and resisted outsiders from the United States and France. The Chinese had historically dealt with competing ethnic groups or clans wanting to subdue their villages, while Africans almost daily battled against white people encroaching upon their social space. Contact with different peoples, in short, had conditioned each group to be wary of outsiders, and as if by instinct, to trust only the familiar.

But, ever ready to contend with the contingency of the moment, the three groups made necessary and appropriate adjustments and compromises to the setting before them, negotiating an accommodation with the social environment. Previously, each had accepted reconciliation with competitors either because dominant societies had forced them to accept new trappings or influential classes had inculcated their own manner of conduct upon the disadvantaged. Adaptation had also resulted from the need to accept survival skills from superior powers, from a certain admiration the oppressed harbored for the oppressor, or from an honest belief common folks held that mainstream institutions were ones to uphold and emulate. In the West, Africans, Chinese, and Mexicans similarly negotiated the minefields of the racial frontier by trying to find their niche through accommodation. Incorporation into the political, economic, and social systems of the West was a desired goal for most, and many committed themselves to learning and accepting the tenets of the land to achieve it.

Some individuals would not let their background, race, or ethnicity place them at a disadvantage when necessity commanded them to approach the political system about personal, even private, wrongs. Slaves theoretically had little knowledge of the law, yet in Texas the freed people during Reconstruction quickly looked toward the Freedmen's Bureau as an institution able to protect rights and privileges for black families. Emma Hartsfield, among many other African American women in Texas, knew enough of the post–Civil War political structure to recognize that the bureau could be an agent in arbitrating matters involving cohabitation. As did others who had lived with men but had not married them (Texas law did not recognize black marriages until 1870), she argued that cohabitation with a man earned certain rights. Thus did Hartsfield visit the Freedmen's Bureau office in Austin in 1867, complaining of deception on the part of her common-law husband, a white man named Lacy McKenzie, who allegedly promised her a house and property if she would live with him. McKenzie, however, reneged on his promises when Hartsfield announced that she was with child; he first desired that she seek an abortion, then attempted the drastic step of disposing of their home and land lot. With the help of the bureau, Hartsfield retained a lawyer and successfully prevented McKenzie from selling their possessions. In fact, she got from her erstwhile mate a parcel of land with two houses on it.[31]

CHAPTER 2

Citizens or Outsiders?

To the Mexican Inhabitants of the STATE OF TEXAS!!!

Mexicans! *When the State of Texas began to receive the new organization which its sovereignty required as an integral part of the Union, flocks of vampires in the guise of men, came and scattered themselves in the settlements, without any capital except the corrupt heart and the most perverse intentions. . . . Many of you have been robbed of your property, incarcerated, chased, murdered, and hunted like wild beasts, because your labor was fruitful, and because your industry excited the vile avarice which led them. . . .*

Mexicans! *. . . On my part, I am ready to offer myself as a sacrifice for your happiness; and counting upon the means necessary for the discharge of my ministry, you may count upon my cooperation, should no cowardly attempt put an end to my days.*

This undertaking will be sustained on the following bases:

FIRST: *A society is organized in the State of Texas, which devotes itself sleeplessly, until the work is crowned with success, to the improvement of the unhappy condition of those Mexican residents therein; exterminating their tyrants, to which end those which compose it are ready to shed their blood and suffer the death of martyrs. . . .*

THIRD: *The Mexicans of Texas repose their lot under the good sentiments of the governor elect of the State, General Houston, and trust that upon his elevation to power he will begin with care to give us legal protection within the limits of his powers. . . .*

COUNTY OF CAMERON CAMP AT THE RANCHO DEL CARMEN,
November 23, 1859 JUAN N. CORTINA

—JERRY D. THOMPSON, *ed.,*
Juan Cortina and the Texas-Mexico Frontier, 1859–1877

Thus spoke Juan Nepomuceno Cortina, then at the head of a Tejano uprising along the Texas-Mexico border. Cortina seems a most unlikely person to have put faith in the American political system, if scholars look no deeper than the superficial portraits generally painted. One school of historians has portrayed him as a *caudillo* (regional strongman) out to build a power base for himself in South Texas, an opportunist who played politics on both sides of the border, a rogue out on a personal vendetta against a handful of Anglos in Brownsville, and a scoundrel who could not possibly have trusted Governor Sam Houston. Others see him as a daring vaquero bold enough to take on the "gringo" system, a son of Mexico's Far North bent on ousting the Anglo invaders, or a revolutionary strident in gaining justice for fellow Texas Mexicans.

Cortina may have combined attributes of both caricatures, but the facts known about his early life make plausible his leadership of a popular uprising in the name of democracy. He was no stranger to the U.S. political system implanted on South Texas by Anglo settlers following the U.S.-Mexico War. Born in Tamaulipas in the year 1824, his initial experience with politics probably paralleled that of other frontier people of the Mexican North, often neglected by the political parties in the interior, yet resilient enough to form their own democratic notions of governance. Such an ethos, the literature holds, took shape due to the manner in which the pobladores went about fending for themselves: warding off Indian attacks, resolving their own problems in the remote corners of the nation, and providing order in the face of neglect from officialdom in the heartland.[1] In the Far North, indeed, governance until the United States acquired the region fell most frequently to the pobladores themselves. Self-rule nurtured democratic ideals and a nationalist identification with the immediate region.[2]

Though Cortina fought against the Anglo soldiers who invaded southern Texas in 1846, he readily converted to the Anglo American order, engaging, in the words of one scholar, "in the rough-and-tumble politics of Cameron County." He knew some of the local government officials well enough and even had family connections (through cross-cultural marriage) with influential Anglos. His mother, the owner of Rancho del Carmen (located close to Brownsville), apparently made a decent living during the 1850s.[3] Thus, by the time of the so-called "Cortina War" of 1859, he had spent several years operating within the U.S. political structure and did not reject the democratic system outright.

While Cortina was no patriot or high-principled citizen, he (and certainly fellow Mexicanos of the period who supported his rebellion) did hold expectations about what government should be. These expectations derived from ideas that had developed in the Far North under Spain and Mexico, but also from exposure to U.S. rule. Under the U.S. Constitution, people felt entitled to certain rights, to have their lands respected and their lives preserved. But that was not the case, as Cortina's proclamation of September 1859 so caustically noted. Yet, despite the wickedness of those "flocks of vampires," Cortina pledged to ameliorate the condition of "those Mexican residents *therein* [i.e., Texas]" and seemingly pinned his hopes on Houston the Jacksonian to "give us protection within the limits of his power."[4] That relief did not materialize, of course; Cortina himself retreated into Mexico, involved himself in the politics of that country, and died there in the 1890s.

Elsewhere in the West, episodes (both peaceful and violent) involving racial groups wishing to find a niche in the politics of the region would be reenacted a hundredfold. All participants found merits in the constitutional system, construing democracy either in its high ideals or in the populist manner that Cortina purportedly saw it. For many, among them people of color who had left despotic governments behind, the politics of the West theoretically guaranteed them basic human privileges and recourse to the law in case of threat to life and property.

While jockeying for space in the West's political structure, some intrigued for higher stakes since democracy as a humanly constructed system also held out the prize of power and domination. The contest sometimes pitted racial minorities against one another. The Chinese often became victims of discriminatory treatment; they seemed to have been the most despised while at the same time they were largely defenseless. In San Francisco during the era of Reconstruction, for instance, African American leaders in the city came to perceive the Chinese (who then outnumbered blacks ten to one) as an obstacle to their community's march toward political equality, and thus opposed Chinese political empowerment. African Americans resisted liberalizing the suffrage because they feared the rise of Chinese political influence and possible political competition. Further, they resented the limitations placed upon their own political opportunities when whites (the masters of both peoples' fate) lumped them together with the Chinese as citizens unworthy of the ballot. To assert their own merit and press their case for constitutional guarantees, black San Franciscans distanced themselves from the Chinese, claiming the latter had no intention of considering Americanization or making the United States their home and that Asians were heathens incapable of living harmoniously alongside Christian believers. Aside from restricting the franchise, Africans also opposed broad educational opportunities in the city, as talk of schooling for anyone other than the white population invariably included integrating the Chinese, a specter that adversely affected blacks. Again African American spokespersons denounced the Chinese as a people with alien sentiments and as ones of no benefit to the country. Only blacks, as admirers of American government and productive contributors to society, deserved proper schooling for their children.[5]

If African American leaders had as their purpose diluting the competition so as to make political strides (however slight those advances), other players in the West craved more ambitious ends: namely, to retain control over government mechanisms and dominate their rivals. Those best positioned to do that were Anglo Americans. Whites felt no compelling desire to relinquish their supremacy over frontier institutions. They after all had "conquered" the West and considered it a trophy. There existed the need, moreover, for a pliant working force that could bolster the American dominion: people of color represented the most ready supply of cheap labor.

Racist sentiments toward such a subaltern population further roused practices of minority exclusion from positions of authority and influence. Racism evidenced itself in numerous perverse guises: in irrational attitudes, in violence, and in legal restrictions, to name only a few forms. Even before heading to the West, for instance, whites had constructed attitudes toward people of mixed ancestry that augured unluckily for Mexicans. One scholar argues that English people in the American colonies had long formed negative perceptions of Spaniards and Latin American Indians, so that westering whites were predisposed to react adversely toward the pobladores upon encountering them in the Borderlands. Early travelers and settlers into Mexico's Far North similarly saw little to praise in the Hispanic working class: Mexicans did not resemble white men in skin pigmentation (but instead reminded whites of Native or African Americans); they seemed morally defective, lazy, and uncaring about life advancement; they laid but a thin claim to civility;[6] and they apparently possessed almost no skills for competing in the fierce battle for human survival. A passerby in 1859 reported in San Antonio:

> The past and the present have met here, and abide in fellowship—the old and the new live side by side—different races, unlike in origin, government, education, religion, domestic habits and national destiny, constitute the population—neither materially affecting the other; each perpetuating the customs peculiar to them while separate. The Mexican, with his old ideas, plans and ways, all ancestral and superannuated, riding his donkey without a bridle, and peddling sticks and scraps for his daily bread; the inventive, headlong American, full of energy, his hopes always a-head of his business and his gains. The one, stagnant from the dulness [*sic*] of his nature and the misrule of his country, content to live without aspiration or change; the other, strained in every muscle and stretched to his full height,

looking out for "the good time coming," and resolved to go and meet it if it does not come soon.[7]

Whether it was in Texas, Arizona, California, or New Mexico, Anglos considered Mexicans as "greasers" and described them as indolent, depraved, prone to violence, lax in moral standards (including the women, who wore provocative clothing and danced the lascivious *fandango*), and worshipers of a pagan religion. Many considered such traits to be inherent in people of mixed-blood constitution.[8] For those with a stake in white supremacy, politics had to be shielded from decadence and degeneration.

To neutralize their adversaries, segments of the white population resorted to lynching, mob rioting, and more subtle misapplications of the law. Generally, racial minority groups fell under the protection of the legal system, but as is the case in other frontier regions of the world, populations wanting to preserve the status quo turn to capricious means in their treatment of those whom they wish to subordinate and hold powerless. The history of the trans-Mississippi West is replete with such cases.

Juan Moya and two of his sons had the dubious distinction of becoming victims of lynch law in Texas. Born in Goliad to pobladores who settled in Texas during the colonial era, Moya had received land grants from the Mexican government during the 1830s in modern-day Bee and Goliad counties. Then, in the summer of 1874, unknown parties savagely killed Thad Swift and his wife, owners of a ranch in nearby Refugio County, ostensibly to rob them. Suspicion fell upon Swift's ranch hands, many of whom disappeared following the grisly crime, but also upon one member of the Juan Moya family who reportedly had visited the ranch on the day of the slaying. An unwritten code existed in Texas forbidding Mexicans (or anyone of color, for that matter) to be insolent toward white people. Impertinent Mexicans could face anything from a ranting rebuke, a pistol-whipping, or, if the infraction be murder, lynch law. That was the penalty in store for those implicated in the Swift murders. A posse trailed the suspects to the Moya property and surrounded the ranch house, but, encountering fire from the Moyas (who apparently feared that the vigilantes considered them guilty and would dispatch them on the spot), retreated to await reinforcements. Seeing the futility of further resistance when the sheriff of Goliad arrived, Moya and his sons surrendered. Hotheads, however, took the Mexicans from the sheriff and summarily assassinated the old man and two of his sons. The actual killer of the Swifts was later caught and legally hanged.[9]

The victimization of helpless minorities also encompassed mob rioting, and one particular episode of white violence took the life of a Denver laundry worker named Sing Lee. The politics of Denver in 1880 had broadened (as they had throughout the West during that era) into Chinese-hating campaigns, topped with rallies, public meetings, and Sinophobic parades. The local Chinese population had earlier worked as miners and railroad hands, but with the exhaustion of the mines and completion of the railroads, now either ran small businesses or eked out a living taking menial jobs in restaurants and Chinese laundries. For whites, however, the Chinese still represented a threat (if only imaginary) to workers, and it took only a minor row at a local tavern between individual Anglo and Chinese pool players on October 31, 1880, to inflame racial passions. A mob of whites (joined by a few African Americans) invaded Denver's Chinatown forthwith, ransacking laundry businesses (the symbol of the hated Chinese), plundering homes and buildings, and traumatizing Chinese residents. Some of the rioters turned on Sing Lee and dragged him along one of the city thoroughfares, fending off intervention by alarmed whites who feared for Sing Lee's life. Efforts by doctors to save the victim proved futile: his death came "from compression of the brain, caused by being beaten and kicked." Police and volunteer forces finally brought order to Denver, but not justice: a local jury acquitted the men accused of Lee's killing.[10] Rioting as a vehicle for control, of course, did not confine itself to the Chinese. Indeed, rioters also targeted such white groups as labor unionists and religious dissenters. But the Chinese appeared to have been at the center of the most notorious violent episodes in the West. These included the Rock Springs Riot/Massacre of 1885 in Wyoming, the Seattle and Tacoma, Washington, riots of the same year, and the Snake River Massacre in Oregon in 1887.[11]

Lynching and mob riots constituted only two of the illegal options available to men in power wanting to still competition from people of color. Easier to do was perverting the Constitution: that is, interpreting and executing doctrine so as to deny undesirables the document's equal protection. Racist politicians by the early 1850s were doing just that to African Americans, hindering them from a new beginning on the frontier. Oregon, for example, as mentioned in chapter 1, incorporated into its constitution of 1857 provisions that denied blacks immigration into the state (the prohibition lasted until 1926).[12] Legislation intended to allow slave catchers to enter Western regions and retrieve runaway slaves made its way into the law books of some of the western states and territories, especially those close to the Mississippi River. Even faraway California passed its own Fugitive Slave Law in 1852, though antislavery sentiment during the mid-1850s diluted it.[13]

Thus, while slavery was prohibited throughout much of the trans-Mississippi West, westering African Americans (both free and slave) found the institution existing in de facto form—that is, entrenched in a mesh of legal proscriptions. To keep African Americans from possibly mustering their numbers and becoming an electorate capable of questioning their own exclusion from politics, Anglos preserved white advantage by depriving blacks of the suffrage as well as other freedoms.[14] Politicians barred African Americans from owning real estate, entering into marriage with a white person (several of the states passed antimiscegenation statutes), attending school, or gaining access to public places or facilities.[15]

Among the most famous cases of racial discrimination in pre-1865 San Francisco was the one involving Mary Ellen Pleasant, arguably the wealthiest black woman in the city. Notwithstanding her close connection to San Francisco's entrepreneurial elite, she along with two other black women in 1864 encountered racism firsthand when a conductor ejected them from their streetcar seats. Mrs. Pleasant ultimately received remuneration for damages following a successful civil action suit against the streetcar line, but the policy of prohibiting blacks from riding common carriers remained long after.[16]

Additionally, Africans could not serve on juries or have recourse to the courts: statutes refused them the right to testify, save in cases involving another African American.[17] In California, the prohibition against black testimony derived from legislative acts passed in 1851, but also from a legal judgment. In 1852, a San Francisco black barber named Gordon Chase died at his shop following a cold-blooded act by a white murderer, and two witnesses prepared to identify the accused as the offender. But one of those called before the bench, Robert Cowles, was revealed to be one-sixteenth black—this upon the determination of doctors who analyzed hair samples—and thus ineligible to speak under oath. The defendant was nonetheless found guilty on the basis of evidenced provided by the second witness, a white man. As with the case of Mary Ellen Pleasant, it would be years before blacks in California received the right to testify against whites.[18]

These several barriers to African American political equality lingered in varying capacities into the post–Civil War era. Trans-Mississippi West states and territories either kept the old body of laws or selectively repealed some while preserving others.[19] Pressure from the federal government became necessary to end such legal restrictions: an act of Congress in 1862 terminated slavery in Utah; the Fourteenth Amendment (1868) erased the status of African Americans as non-citizens; and the Fifteenth Amendment (1870) granted African American men across the United States the right to vote. Despite such mandates, the trans-Mississippi West often took its cue from Redemptionist Southerners. California, Oregon, Nevada, and Kansas among other states either extended the franchise to blacks reluctantly, or found mechanisms to dilute the power of the black vote.[20] Most, if not all, governments still opposed interracial unions, and even states with small African American populations underscored or passed new antimiscegenation laws.[21]

Jim Crow separation, for all intents and purposes, persisted as a matter of tradition, though no strict segregationist decree spewed from territorial or state legislatures, at least for some years. Segregation in the schools and in public facilities such as barber shops, theaters, and street cars existed, but more on the basis of common practice. Enclaves intentionally designated for African Americans were nowhere to be found legally until the 1870s, not even in Kansas where so much of the West's black population resided.[22] Then, even as it was appearing to many

African Americans that indeed sections of the West were emerging as places of tolerance, segregationist traditions took a turn that mirrored trends in the South. During the 1880s, evidence of segregation as an institutionalized practice began to surface: in Kansas, new court cases followed a pattern of negating the legislature's antidiscrimination law. Statutes passed in the wake of Reconstruction had penalized public establishments or transportation lines for discrimination if they operated under a municipal license. But toward the end of the century, Kansas courts gradually overturned those laws, declaring them unconstitutional.[23]

The universally hailed democratic system that people of color expected would be an improvement over homeland government proved something of a chimera. Anglo Americans, who occupied the most significant and persuasive positions on the frontier, held out against conceding partnership to those believed to be social and racial inferiors. As guardians of law and order, they arrogated to themselves the power to castigate those who challenged white authority: Africans, Chinese, or Mexicans must not kill white people even in self-defense. As capitalists with a need to protect their interests, whites believed it permissible to exploit political advantages: white laborers might trust the jury system to acquit them from transgressions. Taking the law into one's hands, therefore, became a staple of frontier democracy, a breach of justice that alarmed those wary of the use of violence. As the reporter for the London *Times* noted of the anarchy that produced the death of Sing Lee: "With the scenes which I witnessed yesterday still vivid before my eyes, I cannot help thinking how bitter a sarcasm does the conduct of the riotous citizens of Denver pass upon the immortal Declaration of Independence."[24] Of course, whites had no pressing need for using extralegal means to prop up white supremacy. More conventional ways lay at their convenience. Disfranchisement, bossism, Jim Crow legislation, and other subterfuges surfaced as common means to defend and protect the status quo. Democracy in the West thus contained a shadier side; legal contrivance denied undesirables their high hopes for political betterment.

Notwithstanding this reality, the West could be a place of political tolerance. True enough that numerous barriers and legal proscriptions existed to keep some Westerners—namely people of color—outside the pale of decision-making. Yet the frontier hardly closed—in caste-like form—constitutional guarantees solely on the basis of race, color, or cultural difference. Numerous reasons might explain such a paradox. Colonial societies in other parts of the world have routinely conceded quasi-legal status to dependent populations; perhaps white Westerners saw such guarantees as a means of appeasing what might otherwise become a troublesome sector. Also, there resided white folks in the West, as is the case everywhere, who genuinely felt compassion for the oppressed and made common cause with them. This cohort might have included men of the cloth, humanitarians, advocates for the downtrodden, or decent frontier people distressed by political unfairness.

Legalists chagrined at a society that twisted laws to fit its needs at the expense of others certainly constituted this element. During the 1870s and 1880s, for instance, federal district judge Matthew P. Deady of Oregon issued a series of rulings favoring Chinese defendants brought before the court on charges related to mining, contract work, gambling, laundering, and opium smoking. Whether the judge or other defenders of Africans, Chinese, and Mexicans had any significant impact on the way Westerners treated people of color remains doubtful. But for minority groups, the actions of whites like Judge Deady reinforced their trust in a system that could respond to their concerns in ways better than homeland governments.[25]

Yet, it took more than Western tolerance and help from Anglo allies for Africans, Chinese, and Mexicans to pierce the political structure and thereby gain freedoms associated with U.S. law. These minority groups had to change themselves. Old traditions had to be scuttled, and the legacy of rule by a more powerful class, an emperor, or a *caudillo* forgotten. Dropping the old and adopting the new republicanism proved uncomplicated for most. In fact, minorities proved resourceful agents in the process of adaptation.

Strategies in the pursuit of aspirations generally entailed emulating techniques and methods already in use throughout the frontier. In picking the proper approaches to attain political ends, of course, minority groups had a range of choices. At times, calling mass meetings, writing petitions, making speeches, mobilizing the electorate around a particular issue, conducting voter drives, or campaigning for political posts might be appropriate. In particular cases, resorting to the court system seemed most feasible. On still other occasions, joining political factions with ethnic platforms appeared a rational alternative.

African Americans proved as adept as any group in the West at making use of this first strategy; to wit, they employed conventional political tactics that would coax government into addressing black-specific issues. Because slavery throughout the West did not exist in an entrenched form, blacks during the 1850s were able to meet and plan policy to an extent unthinkable in the slave South. To display their disappointment with the prohibition of black testimony, with the interdict on black homesteading on open lands, and with educational discrimination against black children, African Americans gathered in the tradition of colored conventions first held in the free North during the 1810s. From conventions such as ones held in Sacramento and San Francisco in 1855, 1856, and 1857, delegates petitioned the California government to repeal decrees that permitted whites to perpetrate crimes upon them with impunity because black victims could not testify against aggressors. They further expressed their contempt for a state that legally sanctioned their second-class status.[26]

Major figures in some of the antebellum California crusades included Mifflin W. Gibbs, a former antislavery crusader from the North who in 1850 traveled to California in search of gold and a new beginning. Failing to find an El Dorado in the mines, Gibbs entered the apparel line, selling clothing for a while before finding some success as an importer of shoes and boots from the U.S. North and Europe. Resuming his interest in politics, Gibbs in 1851 joined fellow black leaders in publishing strident resolutions attacking the many California anti-African American statutes that stifled black desires for political parity. His political passion led him in 1855 to start publication of the first black newspaper in California (called *Mirror of the Times*) and to become a vocal and influential participant in the colored conventions of 1855, 1856, and 1857.[27] The exertions of Gibbs and fellow black activists finally paid off during the Civil War when California elected a Republican governor in 1862. Immediately, blacks in San Francisco intensified their quest for political rights by organizing the Franchise League. Through it blacks continued to campaign for the repeal of laws against black suffrage and black testimony, and, in 1863, the California assembly approved a bill permitting blacks to testify in cases involving whites.[28]

The Union victory in the Civil War brought higher political expectations to African Americans in those states and territories where their numbers might be mustered into political action. The Radical Republican ideology during Reconstruction, moreover, encouraged black Westerners to think realistically about the prospects of voting, being witnesses in courts, serving on juries, entering any public place, and getting a tax-supported education.[29] Many responded to the appeals of the Republican Party to join party ranks, and indeed an upswing in political animation is evident, part of it to be found in the Plains states. Black politicians in the Plains region politicked for party ideology but also on behalf of the franchise, jury service for blacks, the repeal of antimiscegenation laws, the freedom to buy lands in the public domain, and the prospect of enrolling their children in the common schools. In Kansas, the best known of these black leaders were Charles H. Langston, Ephraim McCabe, and the lawyer John Lewis Waller. In Iowa, Alexander Clark carried the mantle for African American concerns during the 1870s and 1880s: he received the title of "Orator of the West" for his speaking eloquence.[30]

Somewhat of an exception as a voice for black folks was William J Hardin, a gallant spokesperson for black rights during the 1860s through the early 1880s, but whose political career prospered due to remarkable support from white voters. The product of a mixed marriage and well educated by Quakers in his native state of Kentucky, Hardin arrived in Denver, Colorado, during the Civil War. By 1865 he had emerged as a crusader for African American rights in the Colorado Territory, insisting that the franchise be extended to African Americans, that the government ease the prohibition against black homesteading on public lands, and that black children be permitted decent access to public education. His skill at speechmaking, debating, organizing petition drives, persuasive letter writing (he corresponded with members of the U.S. Congress, newspaper editors in the North, and many others), and particularly his ability to influence local political leaders won him important backing from whites. Significant support for racial equality came from the territorial governor and from the major Radical Republican newspaper organs in the territory. Hardin's efforts (and those of his black allies) paid off in 1867, when Congress, in accepting Colorado as a territory, extended the franchise to blacks.[31]

Hardin made a subsequent move to Wyoming in 1873, where he emerged more as a stalwart for the Republican Party platform than for black causes. As in Colorado, he garnered substantial backing from white Republicans and a cross-section of political groups (few blacks lived in Wyoming in that era), and gained a seat in that state's House of Representatives for two terms between 1879 and 1883. Hardin's unusual success in the politics of the West has been attributed by one historian to exceptional competence and an innate congeniality that won over both black and white followers. Whatever the reasons, Hardin's career does illustrate what the frontier could be: a place of tolerance, an environment wherein whites could be less than oppressors, and a setting where high expectations might be within one's grasp.[32]

If blacks had been inspired by post–Civil War radicalism, they faced a letdown by the late 1870s, when (as mentioned earlier in this chapter), conservative Democrats regained control of numerous state and territorial legislatures and the Republican party moved away from championing civil rights. The new governments either reversed earlier gains or diluted civil rights victories. In San Francisco, an early example of such reaction was the California Supreme Court's ruling in 1868 against Mary Ellen Pleasant on an appeal by the railroad company that she had earlier integrated. The Democrat-dominated court judged the earlier damages awarded to Ms. Pleasant extreme, and placed obstacles on the path of integrationists who fancied the desegregation of the railroad lines by resorting to legal channels.[33]

An appeal to the courts was a second viable alternative for people of color bidding for accommodation in the West. The Chinese, the group that on first impression would have relied least on the judiciary, became the system's most frequent users. By the 1850s, there lived in California's Chinese American community several leaders who had acquired a working knowledge of U.S. political institutions and who took steps to improve conditions for fellow Chinese Americans. Reliance on the courts, a choice that increased over time, seems remarkable in light of the fact that in the homeland citizens seldom questioned established politics. To the contrary, the appropriate protocol had been acceptance and submission to the law.[34]

Yet numerous cases exist of Chinese Americans in California (but certainly by no means restricted to that state) who placed faith in judicial institutions, believing these institutions might extend to them the charitableness of U.S. democracy. Among those trusting of the courts were parents wishing enlightenment for their children. So far as many Chinese parents were concerned, they had proven their commitment to U.S. society by paying taxes that went toward funding the common schools; certainly their loved ones deserved some returns. Education for the Chinese was not the norm throughout the West, and the matter had not been much of an issue before the Civil War. But as the number of school-age children increased in the Golden State by the 1870s and 1880s, Chinese parents and Chinese organizations launched determined efforts to secure proper mentoring for youngsters.

Among these individual parents was Joseph Tape—an educated, Christianized, and acculturated Chinese American married to a white women—who in 1884 went before San Francisco school officials to ask that his eight-year-old daughter be permitted enrollment. School officials listened politely to his request but rejected the girl's application, saying that being half-Chinese disqualified her from admittance. Because a federal circuit court had recently ruled that anyone born in the United States (including the Chinese) had the rights of citizens, Mammie Tape's parents (with the help of Chinese societies in San Francisco) hired white attorneys who argued before the San Francisco superior court that U.S.-born Chinese were legally entitled to a public school education. The superior court agreed (1885), satisfied that under the Fourteenth Amendment Chinese children and Mammie Tape, as the daughter of an adult who had staked his future on life in the United States, had the right to public education. The San Francisco school board immediately appealed to the California Supreme Court, only to see the earlier decision by the San Francisco superior court upheld. The determination of Joseph Tape and supporters from the Chinese community produced victory, but only a partial one. The state legislature amended the California school laws to permit the Chinese an education, but in segregated facilities.

Separate but equal education would be the norm for the Chinese in California for decades thereafter.[35]

In their attempt to seek judicial redress against discriminatory legislation, Chinese Americans also chose the wiser course of joining associations or self-help groups and pooling resources. During the 1870s and 1880s, the Chinese Consolidated Benevolent Association of San Francisco (the aforementioned Six Companies; it had among its functions helping immigrants adjust to the United States, preserving peace among Chinese factions in the city, and representing the concerns of Chinatown before mainstream society) acquired counsel on numerous occasions to test local ordinances and even national laws that in their view violated the Civil Rights Act of 1870, the Fourteenth Amendment, and the Burlingame Treaty, and some of the exclusion acts of the 1880s.[36]

One such case financed by the Six Companies involved Chae Chan Ping and touched upon the rights of Chinese as stipulated by treaties and national legislation. When railroad magnates had needed Chinese laborers to complete the construction of the transcontinental railroad lines during the 1860s and 1870s, national politicians had been cooperative in easing immigration from China. The Burlingame Treaty of 1868 recognized the legality of Chinese immigration to the United States (and further assumed that the Chinese in the United States had such rights as the freedom to get an American education),[37] but once the railroads connected the frontier, Westerners had little use for the Chinese. As a consequence of the backlash from labor and racist elements, Congress passed the Chinese Exclusion Act (sponsored by Westerners) in 1882. The act—which incidentally prohibited the Chinese from becoming citizens—prevented Chinese immigrants from entering the United States until 1892. In consideration of the provisions in the Burlingame Treaty, the Chinese Exclusion Act allowed individuals already residing in the United States to acquire a certificate from the U.S. government permitting them to visit China and re-enter the United States.[38] This condition was still unacceptable to influential Westerners, who succeeded in getting Congress to pass the Scott Act in 1888. This piece of legislation ceased the practice of issuing certificates and nullified permissions recently issued, thus denying those visiting China the right to return to their homes or businesses in the United States.[39]

Chae Chan Ping preferred life in the United States and fought to retain that privilege. A resident of California since 1875, Chae Chan Ping had sailed for China in 1887 with return certificate in hand, but upon landing in the Golden State in October 1888 encountered custom officials informing him that under the Scott Act his papers were null and void. Wanting to insure their rights under the Exclusion Act of 1882, the Chinese community in San Francisco hired local white attorneys and moved to have a test case on the matter, but they were disappointed to see the local circuit court uphold the Scott Act.

At this point in 1889, the Six Companies invested close to $100,000 in the case of Chae Chan Ping, hiring more attorneys (one from Ohio and the other from New York) to test the legality of the Scott Act, as it violated the Burlingame Treaty and the provisions of the Exclusion Act of 1882. In *Chae Chan Ping v. United States,* however, the Supreme Court determined that the Scott Act was constitutional and laborers suffering from its provisions had no alternative but to heed them.[40]

A third strategy by which less powerful actors in the West sought to sway political policy appropriate to their concerns was that of advancing ethnic platforms. That was the goal in parts of the New Mexico Territory during the latter 1880s and early 1890s. There poor Hispano farmers battled cattlemen, corporate farmers, railroad lines, timber corporations, and land speculating enterprises encroaching onto their communal lands (such as those that constituted the Las Vegas Grant, which Mexico had given to the pobladores in the 1820s). Disappointed with the territorial courts that did not act expeditiously on the matter of Anglo squatting and the problem of fencing the open lands, desperate Hispanos (most of them *pobres,* poor villagers/farmers) from San Miguel County in northern New Mexico rallied behind a shadowy organization that went by the name of *Las Gorras Blancas* (the White Caps). From about 1889 to 1890, the pobres turned vigilantes and behind masked faces engaged in a "terrorist" campaign that entailed cutting fences, burning ranch houses, destroying the harvests, damaging farm equipment, and killing livestock. In March 1890, Las Gorras Blancas rode brazenly into Las Vegas (the county seat of San Miguel County) and posted a listing of their grievances. The platform *(Nuestra Plataforma)* read (in part):

Not wishing to be misunderstood, we hereby make this our declaration.

Our purpose is to protect the rights and interests of the people in general; especially those of the helpless classes.

We want no "land grabbers" or obstructionists of any sort to interfere. We will watch them.

There is a wide difference between New Mexico's "law" and "justice." And justice is God's law, and that we must have at all hazards.

We are down on the race issue, and will watch race agitators. We are all human brethren, under the same glorious flag.

We must have a free ballot and a fair count, and the will of the majority shall be respected.

Be fair and just and we are with you, do otherwise and take the consequences.

The White Caps, 1,500 Strong and Growing Daily

Juan José Herrera emerged as the leading voice and coordinator of Las Gorras Blancas. Well educated, well traveled (for some time he had lived in Utah and Colorado), well familiarized with U.S. politics, and much in tune with issues relevant to the working poor, Herrera had returned to San Miguel County sometime in the late 1880s as an organizer and recruiter for the Knights of Labor. Astutely manipulating the public's support for White Cap activity, by 1890 Herrera had succeeded in stifling the advances of those whom the poor regarded as land barons and monopolists. By 1890, juries in San Miguel County routinely discharged those indicted for conspiracy with the Gorras; courts sympathized with the aggrieved pobres, while local villagers nodded approval of White Cap attacks.

In the summer of 1890, Herrera and his advisors made a calculated decision to switch from confrontational tactics to mainstream politics in order to gain redress from a democratic system they accepted and counted on. They turned to *El Partido del Pueblo Unido* (the United People's Party), a fledgling political faction in San Miguel County advancing an ethnic plank. Posing as a reform alternative to the Democrats and

Republicans, *El Partido del Pueblo Unido* incorporated White Cap expectations even as it attracted such disparate elements as middle-class Hispanos, disillusioned bosses (both Anglos and Mexicans), lawyers, and merchants, as well as Anglo laborites, all of whom now ostensibly shunned the two major parties. It defended the pobres' stand on land and supported their condemnation of machine bossism; they maintained that the latter, in conjunction with the land barons, explained community dispossession. The results in the year's election proved encouraging, as El Partido won every office it pursued and even sent representatives to the territorial legislature. Running on a similar pro-pobre, anti-monopolist platform in 1892, El Partido once again achieved victory, though not as overwhelmingly as two years earlier.

Over the long haul, El Partido could not maintain its momentum and success. Party officials fell into internecine intrigue and personal agendas. The pobres, who made up the bulwark of El Partido del Pueblo Unido, felt betrayed by professional politicians (including fellow Hispanos) who failed to understand their predicament. The land question came to be bogged down in litigation, a process starkly removed from the old more tangible approach of direct action. During the 1890s and early 1900s, Hispanos occasionally found sympathy in the New Mexico courts, but generally decisions were to their great detriment.[41]

Aside from employing methods common to political tradition, using the courts, and looking at alternative political platforms, minorities also utilized unconventional approaches to defend themselves as permitted by the political "code of the West." A standard argument advanced by historians holds that people of color in the latter decades of the nineteenth century felt it perilous to resist violently. The wisest course was not to rock the boat, for their well-being depended on the willingness of whites to tolerate them economically. Murder, boycotts, ostracism, and deportation could well result from impudent behavior.[42] While such a portrayal might apply to the group at large, there were many who individually defied the image of the stoic or passive "sambo." In the Rocky Mountain region, for instance, some Chinese moved about with revolvers hanging from a gun belt. As was the case with other men on the frontier, armed Chinese might turn to the six-shooter to settle personal scores with each other, if not with white settlers, where circumstances dictated standing up for principles.[43]

In what ways, then, did people of color affect politics on the frontier? They made themselves a visible element in the body politic by their insistence that they be acknowledged as legitimate members of the political structure. They carved a place for themselves in the political history of the West, appearing as actors on the campaign trail, in the courts, and on the ballot. Ethnic/racial issues or platforms etched themselves onto the politics of the trans-Mississippi West, as Africans, Chinese, and Mexicans raised questions about their oppression, disfranchisement, or desire for political representation. Multiracial politics did not reach parallel proportions east of the Mississippi River.

Ultimately, however, white Westerners prevailed in the politics of the trans-Mississippi West—not a surprising fact of life, for dominant powers generally reign on frontiers. While the political system of the West recognized freedoms guaranteed under the Constitution, allowed for minorities to engage in political maneuvering, and permitted duly elected minority officials to assume office, the vested interest of whites was not in permitting political equality to people they deemed un-American. The balance sheet indicates that in broad terms, minorities never came to constitute a powerful voting bloc, to rise to an influential constituency, or effectively to force whites to deal with uniquely racial issues. Africans, Chinese, and Mexicans in the last half of the nineteenth century lived in a Jim Crow environment and, as a group, were unable to rise above their relegation to second-class citizenship.

CHAPTER 3

Quasi-Chattels, Coolies, and Peons

[The Chinese] soon flocked into the mining regions in swarms, well satisfied to work over the old abandoned claims left and deserted by others. They were welcomed by the mining communities with open arms, as it was soon discovered that the Chinese would not preempt or locate any new mining grounds, desiring only to buy at a fair price the old work-out claims which had been abandoned . . . and well did these disciples of Confucius merit the title of scavengers of the mining regions, for many of the old claims which had been abandoned as worthless, were not so in fact, as it was soon discovered that from many of them the Chinese were taking out large amounts of gold.
—*Tricia Knoll*, Becoming Americans: Asian Sojourners, Immigrants, and Refugees in the Western United States[1]

The person commenting on this spectacle in 1890 could well have spoken of any pioneer out West toiling to achieve a dream well-nigh elusive in the homeland. The miners to whom he referred had crossed an ocean, but in the trans-Mississippi West they mixed with scores of other workers from different regions and shores, all believing the frontier a fulcrum for opportunity. The "scavengers" noted by our impressionable observer might have been any one of several ethnic or racial groups determined to break from homeland despair and uncertainty. Just as easily, he was describing people of rugged countenance, lured west by a seductive economic system that promised to jump-start their quest for personal improvement and material achievement. Capitalism had its exploitative dimensions, to be sure, yet thousands saw virtue in it and sought gain from it. Unique was the group in the trans-Mississippi West that introduced radical economic philosophies as alternatives. Even unionizing efforts that surfaced as part of labor movements had as their intent extracting from the economic system, not destroying it. Sweeping the mines for gold residue appeared to many to be less than cost effective (and illustrated the deplorable nature of capitalist oppression), but to less fortunate workers such as the Chinese, leftovers symbolized only one of the myriad ways by which the U.S. economy could contribute to individual amelioration and well-being.

Without doubt, the frontier did offer reasonable expectations for rising above the dismal state of living abandoned at the point of origin. Into the West, people (such as those that amazed the California commentator quoted above) could import numerous types of work experiences, put into play their own uncanny knack for creating work where none seemed possible, or apply an ingrained work ethic to job opportunities likely to be underappreciated or rejected by those with a material edge. At the very minimum, these attributes allowed men and women who had the temperament for sacrifice to care for loved ones and create an aura of hope for the young. For pioneers with visions of grand achievements and high goals, the capitalist system and the West's vast natural resources were the stuff that generated mighty profits.

Success also depended on eviscerating or at least disabling others in the competition for profits, status, or simply a living wage. In Arizona, for instance, Spanish-language newspapers assailed Chinese railroad hands laying track near Clifton, with one of them, *Las Dos Repúblicas* of Tucson, ironically announcing Mexicans ready to assume the same job for "salaries as low as generally paid the Chinese." But even unattractive low-paying enterprises like laying track made life passable, and in Arizona during the 1880s the rivalry for these remnants produced tragic racist attacks by Mexicans on competing Chinese railroad laborers. One of those notorious episodes occurred in Calabasas in 1882 and involved a motley gang of white workingmen and Mexican would-be *traqueros* (railroad hands) who blitzed and razed a Chinese railroad camp. This assault and other forms of harassment against the Chinese succeeded to the extent that the railroad magnates switched to Mexican, Indian, and white workers, convinced that the Chinese no longer yielded them a profitable margin.[2]

While some elements in the trans-Mississippi region engaged in tugs-of-war over the mere chance to improve living standards, others waged fierce battles for the opportunity to reap high premiums under capitalism. The advantage for harvesting such earnings went to white Americans, many of whom had chanced savings and risked investments in the expansionist push to the Pacific Ocean. Dominating the economic framework was for them an important consideration. To enhance the possibility of personal fortune and insure the continuation of the democratic ideal, railroad and mine investors, land companies, business people, ranchers/farmers, and speculators of varied sorts rang out for armies of laborers. Best suited as a work force might be people under the illusion that the economic system that exploited them could be as generous to them as it was to their benefactors. Also fit to order would be those entering the frontier with inherent disadvantages and thus unable to compete at parity with those in control.

People of color who sought their new start in the West obviously did so at a demographic handicap. Said differently, those who dominated society by sheer numbers had first pick at economic opportunities. Moreover, such folks enjoyed institutional leverage. White settlers often appealed to police or military authorities, or called for government intervention, at a moment when minorities challenged the economic status quo. Superiority in population numbers coupled with state support gave Anglos a potent role in determining which groups made an economic go of it in the West and which ended up occupying a subordinate status.

Such hindrances as described above could well neutralize any powerful will or determination on the part of disadvantaged peoples aspiring to elevate themselves materially on the frontier. But many of them also suffered from inherent disadvantages that foiled their search for fruitful returns. Where inhabitants were foreign born (or, for that matter, stayed aloof from mainstream institutions), they lacked the requisite familiarity with the nuances of the frontier economy to be upwardly mobile or marketable. Being illiterate or lacking English language skills added to their predicament, for it restricted the choices they had in finding the better paying jobs. When Ah Ho arrived in San

Francisco from China in 1873, for instance, she could neither read nor write, and quickly became integrated into a devitalized labor pool that whites exploited for their own financial advancement. Her helplessness was compounded when fellow Chinese (who had either kidnapped her in China or somehow had persuaded her parents to sell her) compelled the bewildered youth to sign (thumb print) an obligation to prostitution. The provisions of the contract called for her to be a prostitute in the employ of one Yee Kwan for a period of four years. In return for those services, Yee Kwan covered the cost of her passage across the Pacific, as well as other expenses incurred in acquiring her as a prostitute. As part of that arrangement, the innocent Ah Ho became a fragment in a some-what complex structure of subjugation by which the dominant society (by acquiescing in what transpired within ethnic/racial enclaves) kept the working-class Chinese community dependent, pacified, and generally enfeebled. Her powerlessness to advance economically was further exacerbated by gender bias, for as a woman she faced the added hurdle of having to conform to patriarchal traditions that relegated women to a cloistered life. Uneducated, illiterate, caught in a web of control, and because of gender unable to sally out into the public in search of another line of work, Ah Ho represented many people of color on the frontier who were kept from the starting line by personal or group encumbrances.[3]

Also deterring weaker groups from achieving material rewards was the nature of capitalism. Unlike the political system, which contained built-in guarantees to prevent inequalities, the frontier economy left people almost helpless and obligated to rely on raw wit. On the frontier, little in the legal framework existed to prohibit those with an upper hand from degrading or exploiting those looking for a chance at survival. In contrast to politics, the world of economics did not consider whether a worker was a citizen or not, whether people had the power of the vote, or whether groups could take their grievances before the courts.

Further hampering people of color in the race for economic well-being was their relative inability to prevent Anglos from using the strategy of divide and rule. To begin with, Anglos reserved the best employment for themselves: even in the dangerous mines and on the mountain cliffs of a passing railroad line, whites served as supervisors and assigned the least desirable and lowest paying duties to minority groups. Then, Anglos cleverly picked and chose their laborers from the several competitors. They preferred Chinese for railroad work, Africans for low-grade service jobs in the larger cities, and Mexicans for agriculture and ranching. Such preferences generally revolved around popular notions as to who was especially suited for a particular type of occupation, or who could do the work for the cheapest wages. But whites also meant to keep the oppressed at some distance from one another, lest they question white dictates over jobs and wages. Unable to unite along class lines, therefore, people of color sought their livelihood out West at still another unfortunate disadvantage.

Anglos further undergirded their power over Africans, Chinese, and Mexican workers by a crafty use of other options, among them utilizing political clout. While the entrepreneurial corps in the West remained bound to recruiting and exploiting cheap labor, segments of the white working class saw the commitment as a detriment to their individual quest for economic security. This concern becomes clear in the case of Wong Suey Wan, who in 1883 began, in Santa Cruz, California, the courtship of a young white girl named Sarah Burke. When the two married in 1883, it caused near-hysteria within the Anglo American community, with some speculating on the possible forces that led Sarah Burke to make what seemed an insane decision. The editor of the local newspaper some time later blamed the unfathomable attraction on drugs: "This one instance of the debauchery of a white girl through the devilish arts of the opium dens, causes a shudder to run through the community." The union of a "Chinaman" and a white girl only enraged the passions whites already held against the Chinese. On the political front, they swiftly added another pretext for ridding Santa Cruz of the Chinese.[4]

For some years before Wong and Sarah became involved, white workingmen in the town had engaged in political crusading designed to enhance their own economic position. In 1877, a Santa Cruz Caucasian Society had been established in the community. Determined to keep the area white, the association had called upon employees for a boycott of Chinese workers. The next year, local citizens founded a branch of the statewide Workingmen's Party and made a "No Chinaman Need Apply" rhetoric part of their 1878 campaign plank. The town of Santa Cruz soon came under the spell of the new nativism, passing several anti-Chinese laws such as ones prohibiting gambling and others regulating Chinese laundries. The marriage of Wong Suey Wan and Sarah Burke in 1883 only exacerbated local race relations, for there soon surfaced the Santa Cruz Anti-Chinese Association, which launched a "Chinese Must Go" campaign by endorsing an ordinance to remove the Chinese from Santa Cruz. Ultimately, neither racial denunciation nor political agitation by Anglo workers succeeded because Santa Cruz desperately needed cheap Chinese labor. But the upshot of Wong Suey and Wan Sarah's marriage (they went on to have children) had been to fuel the contention that Chinese depressed wages and that something ought to be done politically to eliminate them as economic rivals.[5]

Anglos went beyond agitation in their attempts to dilute the labor competition, for as the effort to enact an anti-Chinese ordinance in Santa Cruz indicates, whites readily aligned themselves with lawmakers if necessary. Territorial and state legislators became willing accomplices in these designs to prevent people of color from sharing in the West's plentifulness. Thus did white forty-niners during the California gold rush elicit the help of the California statehouse to expel Mexicans from the goldfields. The result was the Foreign Miners' Tax Law of 1850, which imposed on non-citizens a monthly fee of $20 for permission to work the diggings. At heart was the tenet that the frontier belonged exclusively to white pioneers and that those of color (even if native born) had no right to its largesse (though the law actually had as its expressed intent raising money for the public coffers). One T. Butler King grumbled that "more than fifteen thousand foreigners, mostly Mexicans and Chilenos, came in *armed bands* into the mining district, bidding defiance to all the opposition, and finally carrying out of the country some twenty millions of dollars' worth of gold dust. [It] belongs *by purchase* to the people of the United States."[6]

With the Foreign Miners' Tax Law as their legal justification, Anglos took voluntary action to oust foreigners who could not verify payment; in most cases, receipts proved of no value to Mexican miners. In the short run, the Foreign Miners' Tax Law miscarried. Too many Californios and Mexicans left the diggings, much to the disappointment of government officials who consequently derived little revenue from the impost, and to the dismay of town merchants who could not survive without the "foreigners" spending capital. The mercantile class had the law repealed by 1851, but it became a prototype of sorts, as whites subsequently resurrected it in California, then copied the law in Washington, Oregon, and Idaho to discourage competition from Chinese miners.[7]

The onslaught upon the Mexican miners coincided with a legal attack on property held by California Mexicans. For years, if not decades after the U.S.-Mexico War, federal authorities asked the Californios to confirm ownership of their real estate. Specifically, the Land Law of 1851 requested that the Californio landowners go before a three-person board (which grantees believed not to be impartial) and authenticate their holdings. Many times unable to provide proper documents, to afford to pay lawyers to defend old claims, or even to travel to San Francisco where the commission held its hearings, many of the rancheros faced victimization by shameless speculators possessing the means to acquire their fertile estates. One historian estimates that almost 40 percent of the land the grantees held before the conquest was lost due to the adverse repercussions of the Land Law of 1851. Those able to escape the complexity of the Land Law still had to deal with other Anglos coveting the old grants. These included unscrupulous attorneys accepting land for legal fees, speculators after lands foreclosed by sheriffs when owners could not pay their taxes, tenacious squatters determined to take advantage of the intricacies of the legal system, or politicos capable of manipulating the power structure for self-aggrandizement.[8]

Whites further hamstrung minority laborers by offering wages so low as to almost insure worker impoverishment and disadvantage. Several factors set the wage scale for Africans, Chinese, and Mexicans. The supply and demand of the marketplace certainly determined salaries, as did the degree of skills required for particular jobs. Racist reasoning undeniably influenced the subsistence wages paid to minorities, as whites tended to believe that those of color were almost divinely meant to work for inhuman pay. Throughout the West, nation builders turned to nonwhite laborers as ideally suited for the development of entire regions. In South Texas following the Civil War, publicists advertised the presence of

Mexican field laborers in glowing terms. A journalist from the lower Rio Grande area in 1877 wrote: "This is a good point to procure Mexican labor, good ranch hands with families may be had for eight or ten dollars per month with board, or they will find themselves and families for from twelve to fifteen dollars, per month with shelter." Another newspaper from Corpus Christi followed in 1885: "Soil and climate are suitable and cheap labor is at hand. Mexican farm labor can be utilized in the culture of cotton as well as during the picking season."[9]

Low wages also resulted from racist assumptions that Mexicans required little compensation for their livelihood, that Mexicans would only squander away hard-earned wages on fun and frolic, and that Mexicans lacked the same work ethic as whites. The journalist J. Ross Browne, visiting the Mowry Silver Mines near present-day Santa Cruz, Arizona, recorded:

> The citizens of Santa Cruz, who are not proverbial for energy, seem to be inspired with new life on occasions of this kind [payday], and never fail to visit the mines in large numbers for the purpose of participating in the general rejoicing. For two or three days the whole hacienda presents a lively and characteristic scene. Work is out of the question [on payday], so far as the peons are concerned. Under the shade of every tree sits a group of thriftless vagabonds, conspicuous for their dirty skins and many-colored serapes, shuffling the inevitable pack of cards or casting their fortune of greasy "hobes" upon the capricious hazards of monte. The earnings of the month are soon disposed of. The women and children are left dependent upon new advances from the store-houses; the workmen are stupefied with mescal and many nights of debauch; and when all is over, the fandango at an end, and the monte tables packed up, every miner bankrupt, and no more goods or money to be had, the posse of sharpers from the border lines of Sonora take their leave.[10]

The result of these perceptions was a low wage scale for most working-class minorities, a custom of economic discrimination evident in the practice of giving higher pay to whites performing identical work as

Africans, Chinese, and Mexicans. On the Arizona frontier, as was probably the case elsewhere, for instance, mine owners paid white laborers $30 to $75 monthly for doing what Anglos contemptuously considered "Mexican work." Such tasks involved using the pick and shovel for carrying ore; for such chores, Mexicans got $12.50.[11]

Numerous other mechanisms served whites in deterring people of color from the chance at fulfilling their expectations on the frontier. The threat of dismissal from the job, the use of violence, and the debt at the company store all achieved the desired effect: preventing minorities from becoming viable economic rivals. Money owed to the company store, for instance, prevented Mexican miners from leaving the worksite in search of better options. These and other techniques also immobilized those employed by ranches and farms, the railroad lines, and even urban businesses.[12]

Whites also joined labor unions with a clear aim to maintain their edge over competitors. Anglo Americans had the advantage of race in beating out people of color for certain jobs, but that advantage escalated when white workingmen put up a united front in vying for particularly skilled and desirable occupations. All-white unions generally fell back on a range of tactics: one strategy demanded that employers release minority workers, as whites would not work alongside those of color. More ominously, craftsmen could just set their sights on displacing skilled or experienced minority workers, as happened in San Francisco at the Palace Hotel in 1889.[13]

Since 1875, this extravagant and elaborate establishment—in catering to a largely wealthy white clientele—had employed a largely African American kitchen, dining room, and hotel staff. During the latter 1880s, however, white cooks and waiters (who in 1883 had founded a "protective and benevolent" union to represent their interests), began maneuvering to acquire the lucrative positions available at establishments such as the Palace. Apparently, the Cooks' and Waiters' Union successfully negotiated an arrangement with the new Palace ownership in 1889, for almost immediately upon taking over, the new management released its black waiters, accusing them of malfeasance on the job. A few days later, the African American kitchen/dining room staff followed the hapless waiters into unemployment, and eventually so did African American bellboys and porters, all of them replaced by white help.[14] As with other people of color throughout the West, the job security of the experienced and highly regarded African American staff at the Palace hinged precariously on the goodwill of white employers. Lamentably, the recourses available to minority peoples when faced with political injustice—such as turning to the courts, or organizing for self-protection—did not avail themselves as appropriate choices in the economic sector.

The system that promised so much let down those of color who clutched genuine hopes and expectations for material gain. At almost every turn, whites placed high hurdles before the African, Chinese, and Mexican dream of improving upon the standard of living left behind in the homeland. Political maneuvering kept minorities off balance as they looked for an equal chance at moneymaking. Trying to wrest a competence by taking dangerous and low-paying jobs only enhanced the fortunes of whites while leaving minorities to face familiar impoverishment.

The timely use of devices such as the company store helped maintain for whites a convenient work force of quasi-chattels, coolies, or peons. Labor organizing, which generally excluded minorities, had among its results keeping Africans, Chinese, and Mexicans relegated to the lowest plane in the occupational hierarchy. For so many out West, capitalism came to represent despair more than hope. The frontier economy could as readily break the spirit of workers as enrich them.

Despite its seemingly rigid nature, the frontier economy never closed every possible opportunity for personal advancement, and Africans, Chinese, and Mexicans (generally as individuals) found cracks in the system and achieved tangible rewards. Several factors might account for such apertures in an otherwise intransigent system. People with abstemious habits, patience, or economic acumen have universally been able to prosper despite the circumstances of the moment. Members of the oppressed served as intermediaries with the colonized working class, and white society may have acquiesced at the presence of such a fledgling group within ethnic/racial enclaves. As was the case with politics, Anglos at times needed Africans, Chinese, and Mexicans as partners in certain moneymaking ventures, and minorities profited on those occasions.

One historian has noted the case of Nicodemus, Kansas, in the years 1887–1888 as one example of such an interracial economic alliance. There, in a period of several months, the predominantly black commercial class (which had dominated the town ever since the settlement's founding in 1877) and the white business elite rallied to entice the railroad line into passing through the city. For the time, racial prejudice was suspended as the two peoples placed priority on the community's prosperity and the financial good of the entrepreneurial class. Unfortunately for Nicodemus, the railroad company bypassed the town in favor of a neighboring community.[15]

Similar cooperative situations existed in other parts of the West. One study of the Rocky Mountain region, for instance, finds that during the 1860s through the 1880s, Chinese miners lived well materially, working as they did in an area where cordial race relations, available opportunities, and a tolerant legal system were the norm. Whites in the Boise Basin hoped their Chinese neighbors would help bolster the local economy and augment revenue by the taxes they paid. White and Chinese merchants also worked harmoniously in this isolated frontier setting.[16]

But economic improvement in the West involved more than having a talent for self-advancement, luck at becoming part of a "privileged" sector, or getting assistance from empathetic white capitalists. Also required were a dutiful approach to work, the ability to learn new trades, the dexterity to fill professional positions as they appeared, the aptitude for applying old work experiences to the new job situations, the genius to create new employment opportunities, and the bravado to strike against the boss man when working conditions became unbearable. In taking such initiatives, people of color helped themselves, but, equally significant, also added a multicultural dimension to the flowering of the trans-Mississippi frontier.

Striving for a livelihood out West certainly demanded a tough work ethic, and from time to time employers spoke in very glowing terms about the job performance of those they exploited. "Diligent," "hardworking," "enterprising," and "law-abiding" were among words used to label Chinese crews working the railroad lines, the mines, the farms, or the urban factories, for instance. In the words of one early historian, at least some Westerners who employed Chinese considered the Asians "industrious, quick to perceive and understand, tractable, inoffensive, and willing to undertake hard, disagreeable, and menial labor." That regimen was among the factors that led white workingmen to dislike the Chinese and produced the aforementioned "back to China" incentive.[17]

Knowledge of railroad track laying was not something the Chinese imported, but they were quick studies and soon learned much about its operation, including grading, digging tunnels, covering up swamps, building bridges, and handling explosives. Their value was first dramatized after the Civil War, during which the Central Pacific Railroad had begun building from Sacramento and was to weave its way through the Sierra Nevada and into Utah, where it would meet the Union Pacific Railroad coming from the east. When in 1865 it became evident that a labor shortage existed to staff the line, the Central Pacific commenced experimenting with Chinese laborers, hiring as many as ten thousand to eleven thousand (or about four of five) to do the Herculean work needed to overcome the hazards of the Sierra Nevada.[18]

As others of the working class have done universally in their intent to further themselves and loved ones substantially, the Chinese undertook daring tasks while under the employ of the Central Pacific, earning a deserved distinction for bravery and courage beyond the call of duty. According to well-known lore, Chinese laborers working on the Central Pacific in the spring of 1866 risked death at Cape Horn Mountain in the Sierra Nevada by allowing fellow workers to ease them down cliffs on wicker baskets tied to ropes. Their task entailed placing dynamite on the mountain edges, then gambling that their countrymen could hoist them up before the explosives detonated. This daredevil feat begot the phrase "not a Chinaman's chance."[19]

During the winter of 1866–1867, the general superintendent of the Central Railroad, Charles Crocker, ordered his Chinese crew to start tunneling through Donner Summit in the high Sierra. Already contending with ominous obstacles, the Chinese had to work through a terrible winter of high snowdrifts that compelled them to build living and working accommodations under the snow. A veritable maze of underground passages resulted: the Chinese formed small camps wherein they ate and slept, never seeing the light of day but using candles to make their way around their improvised village and guide themselves to work. Undaunted by conditions, they daily burrowed through the mountain with pick and shovel, blasting at critical points along the way and dutifully removing the debris. Several cave-ins occurred, killing an unknown number of Chinese, before the winter mercifully ended. But the excavation of Donner Summit continued during the spring of 1867, and according to Crocker, who years later detailed working conditions during that and the following winter:

> [The Chinese] are equal to the best white men. We tested that in the Summit tunnel, which is in the very hardest granite. We had a shaft down in the center. We were cutting both ways from the bottom of that shaft. The company were in a very great hurry for that tunnel, as it was the key to the position across the mountains, and they urged me to get the very best Cornish miners and put them in the tunnel so as to hurry it, and we did so. We went to Virginia City and got some Cornish miners out of those mines and paid them extra wages. We put them into one side of the shaft, the heading leading from one side, and we had Chinamen on the other side. We measured the work every Sunday morning; and the Chinamen without fail always outmeasured the Cornish miners; that is to say, they would cut more rock in a week than the Cornish miners did, and there it was hard work, steady pounding on the rock, bone-labor. The Chinese were skilled in using the hammer and drill; and they proved themselves equal to the very best Cornish miners in that work. They are very trusty, they are very intelligent, and they live up to their contracts.[20]

In mid-1868, the Chinese finally bored through the Sierra and continued east to Utah.[21]

Once the Central Pacific met with the Union Pacific at Promontory Point near Ogden, Utah, in 1869, the Central Pacific released its workers, and some of these rail men applied their skills to railroad building elsewhere in the West. Recent arrivals from the homeland and transfers from other jobs joined the veteran track men during the 1870s and early 1880s to find work on the Southern Pacific Railroad that connected Los Angeles, Arizona, and Texas. Others helped lay track for the Union Pacific Railroad in southwest Wyoming during the 1870s, as well as for other lines such as the Northern Pacific Railroad that during the 1880s crossed Washington, Idaho, and Montana (approximately fifteen thousand, or three-fourths of the work force on the Northern Pacific, were Chinese). Lines in Oregon and Washington State also hired Chinese migrants during the 1880s.[22]

When occupations requiring more than simple brawn surfaced on the frontier, minority groups stood prepared to assume the important responsibilities attached to them. Slaves had helped in the protection of the trans-Mississippi West before the Civil War by assisting in the building and maintenance of frontier garrisons, for instance. During the war itself, African Americans in Kansas contributed to Union battlefield forces by performing guard duty and building fortifications.[23]

Then, in 1866, Congress passed legislation creating six regiments of black soldiers (four infantry, two cavalry) for duty on the frontier and in the South, thereby affording blacks opportunities to join the military not only as a commitment to the defense of their country, but as a means of human survival. This legislation, and a subsequent law in 1869 that reduced the number of black infantry units to two, produced the rise to distinction of the noted "Buffalo Soldiers"—so named by Native Americans in the West who compared the black men's hair with that of the buffalo— in the last decades of the nineteenth century. Black troopers received assignments to areas of the trans-Mississippi region that included Texas and the Southwest, Kansas, the Dakotas, and Utah, among other states and territories.[24]

Black military personnel executed a wide variety of tasks, from performing routine chores around garrisons to searching for lawbreakers; patrolling the border and scouting the frontier; protecting settlements, ranches, farms, and civilian workers; escorting freighting outfits; laying roads; linking telegraph lines; and engaging in the "Indian Wars" of the 1870s and 1880s.[25] In this latter capacity, seventeen Buffalo Soldiers (of a total of twenty-three recipients) earned Medals of Honor in the West. Two of these (Sergeant Moses Williams and Private Augustus Walley) won their hero's medal in the same battle: against the Apache Chief Nana, a Victorio associate. The two men belonged to I Troop of the Ninth Cavalry, a detachment (then under the command of Lieutenant George R. Burnett, a white officer trained at West Point) assigned to patrol duty in the New Mexico Territory. In August 1881, the company responded to the pleas of a distraught Mexican whose entire family had just been massacred by Nana and his warriors.

With a following of approximately fifty men (including about sixteen Buffalo Soldiers and several Mexican American volunteers), Burnett caught up with and trapped Nana and perhaps sixty other Apaches in the rocky terrain at the base of Cuchillo Negro Mountains. But the Indians held an elevated position permitting them the advantage over their pursuers, and after several hours of desperate hostility, Burnett ordered a retreat. Three men unable to hear the order remained behind, however, still ducking firepower. Determined to rescue their beleaguered comrades, Burnett, Williams, and Walley launched a daring sortie. Walley, exhibiting great courage, rode toward the besieged soldiers, mounted an injured trooper on horseback, and whisked him away from the hellish scene. Burnett and Williams, meantime, got caught in heavy rifle fire, but both were crack marksmen and responded with expert gunplay of their own, enabling the other two soldiers to make it out of harm's way. At nightfall, Nana inexplicably left the battleground and rode off into the mountains. In his report, Burnett praised the valor of his entire company, recommending some for certificates and others for Medals of Honor. Walley received his Congressional Medal in 1890, Williams in 1896, and Burnett—himself recognized for similar bravery—got his own Medal of Honor in 1897.[26]

Whatever their point of origin, pioneers brought diverse work experiences from the homeland and applied them functionally to the frontier. Mexicans, for instance, held much knowledge of mining. Those immigrating from states such as Sonora, Chihuahua, and Durango in Mexico were especially well acquainted with the industry, and historians are all too familiar with the numerous contributions Mexicans made to the mining West. It was Mexicans in the 1850s who introduced approaches toward placer mining, specifically the use of the *batea* (a pan or tray) in working the diggings of particularly dry areas in southern California (the general lack of water there compelled gold seekers to rely on this method of heating the gold and sand, then separating the gold by blowing off the unwanted debris from the batea).[27] Mexicans also transplanted the concept of the *arrastra* used in quartz mining. Some more useful method of crushing the quartz became imperative as California miners struck richer deposits, and the *arrastra* became the most appropriate technique by the 1850s. Improvising, Mexicans found a large stone base, drilled a hole in its middle for a post, and hitched a mule to the pole so that the mule could drag a large granite that ground the quartz. By using quicksilver once the last operation had been finished, miners separated the gold from the pulverized remains.[28]

Work in some of the California mines was every bit as hazardous as that which the Chinese saw in the construction of the railroads during the 1860s and 1870s. In the New Almaden mine—which contained the largest deposits of quicksilver (an ingredient necessary for separating the gold and silver from the ore)—miners during the 1860s performed incredible feats. The journalist Carey McWilliams described work at the mine as follows:

> Living in a town on the hill near the mine, the Mexicans were divided into two categories: the actual miners or *barreteros;* and the ore-carriers or *tanateros.* Starting from the pit of the mine, the ore-carriers would fill a large sack or pannier made of hide with two hundred pounds of ore and then ascend the *escalera* or ladder-like circular path to the surface. Open at the top, the pannier was flung over the shoulder and supported by a strap passing over the shoulders and around the forehead. Ore-carriers made from twenty to thirty trips a day up the escalera for all the ore was carried to the surface by hand. The escalera was narrow, slippery, and lighted only by a few flickering torches.[29]

Numerous range skills that Mexicans had honed during the pre-1848 era also proved useful and applicable in the Anglo American

West. The ability to manage draft animals came to be of much practical utility for Mexicans after 1848, for until the railroads displaced them, arrieros did a good bit of the freighting throughout the Southwest. In Texas before the Civil War, ox-cart commerce was almost the exclusive domain of Tejanos. According to Frederick Law Olmsted, who toured the state during the late 1850s: "The Mexican appears to have almost no other business than that of carting goods. Almost the entire transportation of the country is carried on by them with oxen and two-wheeled carts."[30] Mexican arrieros earned kudos from Westerners for their ability to handle oxen and mule teams and for their success in getting their cargoes through almost any kind of terrain. Throughout the U.S. Southwest they transported clothes, kitchen utensils, supplies of assorted types, and cotton not only to civilian destinations, but to military installations as well.

Mexican miners who joined the gold rush in the Pacific Northwest in the 1850s and 1860s took with them the Mexican pack mule system and developed it into the primary means of transportation for all kinds of cargoes. Mexican packers included the likes of José Montejo, who made his living in the Idaho Territory during the 1870s. Montejo never did accumulate enough capital to acquire a pack train of his own, but like so many other Mexicans working in the industry, he was highly skilled, expert at knowing how to tie down heavy loads to have a minimum impact on every mule, how to traverse dangerous mountain paths, and how to insure his own survival as well as that of his mules while in transit with valuable cargoes.[31] Like Montejo in the Northwest, Mexican freighters elsewhere in the West handled the transportation of goods until the railroad permanently displaced them. In their roles as packers and drivers they became key players in the transportation network, which historians have generally recognized as among the most significant factors enhancing the development of the trans-Mississippi West.[32]

Survival on the frontier also turned on deftness at creating work opportunities within different segments of the economy. In the Rocky Mountain area, and presumably elsewhere in the West, for instance, the Chinese devised innovative marketing techniques in the quest for a decent daily fare. Instead of selling their vegetable produce from stationary posts, as whites did, Chinese vendors picked their vegetables (from their own garden plots) early in the morning and walked house-to-house peddling their harvest. Within a matter of years during the 1870s, they had come to dominate the trade in the Boise Basin of Idaho.[33]

At an individual level, some worked out arrangements with white employers wherein they exchanged their labor for a sense of security and stability. Agustín Quintanilla typified the Tejano ranch hand who worked at the legendary King Ranch during the last decades of the nineteenth century. In the mid-1880s, Quintanilla went to work for Robert Kleberg, the rancho's new owner, who had married into the King family. As a member of the work force on the ranch, Quintanilla provided year-round labor in return for a place to live, the freedom to hunt on the local pasture, and the peace of mind that he could live out his last days at his designated *jacal* at the King Ranch. He also had the privilege of performing duties he felt he did exceptionally well. Quintanilla went on to earn a place in King Ranch lore as a *Kineño* (King Ranch employee) without peer among other equally capable vaqueros. The King Ranch setting was unique among the many ranches that Mexicans worked across the West, to be sure. The symbiotic relationship between *patrón* and vaquero there begot a mutual respect (even though living conditions were only marginally better than those endured by other Tejanos from the lower class), whereas elsewhere on Texas ranches, labor relationships paralleled those found in Western mining or the railroad industry. But as late as the 1950s, the Kineños felt that "they work with the Klebergs, not for them."[34] If fortunate, Mexicans such as Quintanilla could remain on a South Texas ranch for years (and their family perhaps for generations).

Over the last half of the nineteenth century, then, minority groups were not passive historical subjects simply grateful for the opportunity to eke out a bare subsistence. Many had a vested interest in developing the West, as their own hopes for improvement rested on a vigorous and ever-growing economy. Utilizing a work ethic matching that of fellow pioneers, people of color committed themselves to the building of the infrastructure, the exploitation of the region's natural resources, and the advancement of certain industries. They tempted life—by their performance of the most perilous tasks—in the expectation that the frontier would reward them in ways that it did others. The exploitation of the mines and the laying of railroad tracks, for example, cost them thousands of casualties, a fact that few whites disputed.

People of color furthered the frontier by other than casualties. The Chinese, for one, set the model, established the standard, and shaped the work routine during the 1870s for the salmon cannery industry in the Pacific Northwest. One historian graphically describes Chinese cannery workers operating the beginning of the production line.

> The process [of canning the salmon] began with unloading the fish from a scow onto the dock with a "pew," a two- or three-pronged pitchfork-like tool. Either in the scow or on the dock, one or two workers generally sorted the salmon by size, quality, and type. Still others filled two-wheeled carts and took the salmon to the butchering tables.
>
> At the butchering tables, two-man gangs handled the salmon. One worker lifted the fish to the table, and the other removed the fins, tail, head, and entrails. He tossed waste down a chute, or a hole in the cannery floor, to the river below and threw the dressed salmon into a large tub of salt water. Another Chinese worker washed and then scraped the fish with a knife. The latter step, known as "sliming," removed the mucous covering, some of the scales, and any blood or offal from the salmon. A second saltwater bath and another scraping and washing followed. A final once-over with a whisklike brush removed any other foreign matter.
>
> Using a gang-knife with multiple blades, a Chinese worker then cut the salmon into sections the same length as the height of the cans.[35]

In addition, people of color stimulated the frontier economy by purchasing manufactured goods produced domestically or imported from the East, by paying property taxes, and by relying on services available from Anglo professionals. But they furthered growth and progress in a more indirect, though no less important, way: by establishing and nurturing a type of subeconomy. In almost every African quarter,

Mexican barrio, or Chinatown, merchants and professionals pursued the chance to make their living by founding enterprises that would service their own. Racial neighborhoods became commercial zones where ambitious or opportunistic African, Chinese, or Mexican entrepreneurs could try to scratch a livelihood from pursuits denied to them by white merchants and monopolists. Funeral homes, drug stores, mercantile establishments, restaurants, and the like thus appeared as fixtures of almost every racial locale. Women forced by circumstances into prostitution similarly confined their practice to quarters where their own race predominated. Such subeconomies are often ignored completely as historians opt to focus on the more dynamic aspects of the West's broader development. But ordinary folks who spent their earnings in such districts (often because segregationist customs kept them there) advanced the West's economic progress as much as did white people residing in the numerous small towns and isolated villages scattered throughout the West.

In the struggle for life's comforts on the frontier, however, minority groups (while granting that the frontier economy offered greater hope than did the one at home) found "free enterprise" in the West no less callous than politics. In the contention for material betterment, Anglos edged them out. Certainly, white society needed laborers and offered minorities the chance to improve their condition. But the best of opportunities were to be kept at a premium, for it was in the majority's interest not to have colored minorities become potential competitors. In general terms, the latter came to be concentrated in occupations that only bolstered the status quo. Most found it difficult to strike, initiate boycotts, or make demands for fairness on the job site. As racial groups, Africans, Chinese, and Mexicans lived with the stigma of being mainly suited for work of the hardest, dirtiest, and cheapest sort. Racial exploitation for them existed as a grim comparison to the high expectations so many had harbored about reversing their fortunes once entering the trans-Mississippi West.

Poor frontier families had to improvise at house building. Like other settlers in the Plains, the Shores family found shelter in their own sod house. Courtesy of the Nebraska State Historical Society, collection no. RG2608, item no. 1231.

6 Ragsdale.   Photographer.

The Mexican working class made its living in many ways. Sheepshearing was an occupation familiar to Mexican ranch hands. Often sheepshearers traveled from ranch to ranch seeking out this kind of employment in the West. Courtesy of Fort Concho Museum.

Juan N. Cortina led a revolt of Texas-Mexicans in South Texas against Anglo rule in 1859. Many Tejanos thought him a hero; Anglos portrayed him as a rogue. Courtesy of the UT Institute of Texan Cultures at San Antonio, no. 73-842a.

HANGING OF THE MEXICAN WOMAN.

Anglo miners hanged Josefa in Downieville, California, in 1851 for allegedly killing a white miner (the perpetrator had made unwanted advances toward the accused). In Texas, Chepita Rodríguez was executed in 1863, also for allegedly killing a white man. Courtesy of the California History Room, California State Library, Sacramento, California, neg. no. 8735.

The Chinese were the victims of greater racial violence than either Africans or Mexicans. Some of the most notorious "riots" in the West had Chinese as their target. Job competition, nativism, and racism motivated hatred. Courtesy of the Colorado Historical Society.

Though Western communities prevented African Americans from free political participation, a few black politicians rose to prominence. One was William Jefferson Hardin, who (with the support of both black and white constituents) established a successful political record in Colorado and Wyoming in the 1860s through the 1880s. Courtesy of Wyoming State Archives, Department of State Parks and Cultural Resources.

Not too many "clean jobs" existed in the West for African Americans. Among the few were those at hotels, where African Americans worked as part of the dining room staff and as waiters. Some establishments catered to the very affluent, as was the case with the Palace Hotel in San Francisco. Courtesy of the California History Room, California State Library, Sacramento, California, neg. no. 7125.

Kansas in the years after the Civil War became a refuge for African Americans leaving the South. Thousands of people relocated to Kansas and founded predominantly black towns in the late 1870s. One was Nicodemus. Courtesy of the Kansas State Historical Society.

Without any background in railroad building, the Chinese developed expertise in track laying, and found work in many railroad lines in the West. They burrowed through Donner Summit in the winter of 1866–1867 as part of the work crew in the Central Pacific. Courtesy of MSCUA, University of Washington Libraries, neg. no. UW552.

Among the most prestigious jobs for African Americans in the West was soldiering. Several "Buffalo Soldiers" earned Medals of Honor for their role in frontier defense. Courtesy of the Kansas State Historical Society.

The Chinese are credited with having developed the techniques used for canning salmon in the Pacific Northwest. Courtesy of the Oregon Historical Society, neg. no. OrHi24568, #238-A.

Clara Brown won praise in Colorado for her benevolence in behalf of both black and white communities from the 1860s to the 1880s. The Society of Colorado Pioneers honored her in the early 1880s with an invitation to join their all-white society. Courtesy of the Colorado Historical Society.

Mrs. Refugio Amador and her daughters pose for a family picture. The good standing of the Amador family did not spare them the harsh conditions of the frontier. Mrs. Amador ran the family's farm operations and her husband's mercantile establishments during Mr. Amador's frequent absences on business matters. Courtesy of Rio Grande Historical Collections, New Mexico State University Library.

Men primarily constituted the first wave of immigrants coming from China to the United States. Over time, however, women also arrived (albeit in limited numbers) and the result by the last decades of the century were social stability for Chinese communities and families such as that of Jung San Choy. Courtesy of the California History Room, Monterey Public Library, photo no. 4453.

Gender restrictions that existed in the homeland generally were maintained in the West. By the 1880s, however, Chinese women and wives came to acquire new freedoms. They were permitted, for instance, to leave the home and to add to the family income by working as dressmakers or laundresses. Courtesy of Special Collections, University of Nevada, Reno Library, photo no. 1355.

That the West might at times be a place of racial tolerance is seen in the case of Polly Bemis. Bemis, a Chinese immigrant, married Charles Bemis and went on to enjoy an agreeable life at their ranch in Idaho. Courtesy of the Idaho State Historical Society, neg. no. 71-185.29.

This Spanish medieval drama, Los Pastores, was popular among Mexican frontier communities. At Christmas time, Mexican Americans recreated the scene of the shepherds' celebration of Christ's birth. Here the cast poses for a photo. Courtesy of the UT Institute of Texan Cultures at San Antonio, no. 68-533.

Social gatherings such as this one at San Juan, California, around 1880, served the function of strengthening family and community ties. They afforded working families the occasion for leisure in an otherwise trying frontier experience. Courtesy of the Southwest Museum, Los Angeles, photo no. N30590.

The "Watermelon Race" was a popular form of entertainment in Texas.
The sport called for the several contestants to try to carry a watermelon to a finish
line without dropping it. The sport tested riding skills and manual dexterity.
Courtesy of the Daughters of the Republic of Texas Library at the Alamo.

CHAPTER 4

Customs of Color

Poor me! In China I was shut up in the house since I was 10 years old, and only left my father's house to be shut up in my husband's house in this great country. For seventeen years I have been in this house without leaving it save on two evenings (San Francisco, 1893).

—JUDY YUNG, Unbound Feet: A Social History
of Chinese Women in San Francisco

Such sentiments—as uttered by a person who had lived in Chinatown since 1876 as the wife of a well-to-do businessman—attest to the tenacity of customs even after those who imported them had been detached from their homeland for decades. The woman's despair obviously derived from her hopeless life of solitude, but her voice also reflected dismay that the custom would persist eternally, dooming her to a reclusive existence. Her fears, indeed, were well founded, for those who arrived in the West—whether Anglos or Africans, Chinese, or Mexicans—seldom seriously considered cutting links to their parent culture. Most people cherished their customs and traditions out West, regarding them as links to an honored past, and as constituting the fabric of group solidarity and community identity. Certainly every group's culture contained odious customs, but those were often in the eyes of the beholder. Cloistering women seemed no more anomalous to the Chinese than whites enslaving African Americans or exterminating Native Americans.

Universally, people seldom despise the customs of their own land. Rather, they are taught to give homage to their country and praise what it represents: over the generations civilizations endure invasions, wars, famines, revolutions, domestic turmoil, and every imaginable crisis. From these experiences derive a unique national character and psyche, and people form an ethnocentric vision of their country and traditions. All races that met in the trans-Mississippi West to seek a new destiny naturally claimed an exalted, even majestic past, and gave no apologies for their customs and cultural behavior.

In contrast to their view of the West as a setting for new political and economic beginnings, however, those entering the trans-Mississippi West after 1848 saw the frontier as a neutral ground when it came to observing customs and abiding by group attitudes as they always had. In self-contained racial/ethnic enclaves, beliefs about women, for instance, might be heeded and protected. Simultaneously, the customs of "outsiders" might be spurned. In their private arena, Africans entertained no wish to imitate the Chinese, the Chinese rejected Mexican customs, the Mexicans shunned the Saxon heritage, and Anglos saw little of redeemable quality in the ways of Africans, Chinese, and Mexicans.

In reality, no pressing reason existed for Westerners to adopt the customs of opposite others they met in the hinterlands. Appropriate adjustments were made in the work place and in politics, of course, but so little social contact occurred among the races otherwise that each felt no inclination to forsake, for customs they considered problematic, their own norms governing family life, the nuances of social conventions, or ties to community organizations. In the mind of each of the minority competitors on the frontier, their own civilization seemed perfectly satisfactory, especially when measured against that of the whites who mistreated and exploited them shamelessly. Over time, cultural modifications indeed occurred among all involved, but the result would still be a West of many colors.

For minorities, then, living by homeland customs in the West was an agreeable condition. One's traditional lifestyle would best be maintained in segregated racial preserves, even though segregation had abominable implications. In sequestered zones, frontier people observed and de-fended customs unique to their respective pasts. Within segregated areas, furthermore, minorities assumed responsibility for maintaining moral order or enforcing codes of conduct, for generally authorities had little interest in what transpired within those quarters. Communities might act as defenders of their own, for instance, especially of women who caught the eye of male predators, including white men. They could collectively ostracize a criminal element amongst them or those who inclined towards perversion. Child molesters, rapists, or those engaged in incestuous relationships might be tagged as outcasts. Retribution might be taken against those perceived to have malevolent influence or vile powers upon their countrymen.

Antonia Alaniz fell victim to such suspicions, according to the Brownsville *Ranchero,* a border newspaper in pre–Civil War Texas. Antonia had apparently earned a reputation as some kind of sorcerer in the Mexican community of Roma, Texas. Her powers—at least as Antonia's accusers contended—enabled her to cast evil spells on people or to perform devilish deeds. In 1860 she allegedly bewitched a young man named Ambrosio Ramírez, and by having done so, prevented his recovery from syphilis, a sexually transmitted disease. Enraged by the woman's powers, Ambrosio's father, one Matías Ramírez, had the woman kidnapped and then dragged across the Rio Grande into Camargo, where his son then lived. There, for the period of two weeks, Matías's henchmen tortured the victim with beatings and with prickly pear thorns applied to her head, but when these acts ostensibly failed to bring Ambrosio relief, the abductors set the torch to the folk doctor. According to a Camargo medicine man supervising the exorcism, burning her appeared the only recourse, for only as the woman scorched could he remove pigeon bones supposedly lodged in Ambrosio's head. Antonia thus died at the hands of her own people, who believed in the custom of *embrujo* (bewitching) and took it upon themselves to retaliate against the perpetrator, even if by foul and sadistic measures.[1]

Anglo American newspapers were inclined to emphasize depravity in the character of peoples of color, and such a story as the one involving the burning of Antonia Alaniz may have been an exaggeration of events or even a fabrication. Still, ordinary folks on the frontier, irrespective of race, likely brought (or sustained) some acceptance of the paranormal as part of an irreducible culture. Most plain people's customs, however, were much more mundane, as in the case of making social distinctions among themselves. In the homeland, such customs gave reasons and regularity to one's community, and the trans-Mississippi West hardly represented a departure from the norm, as indeed there existed on the frontier a small class of professionals, landowners, government officials, entrepreneurs, and respected individuals worthy of middling and even elite status.

Such a cohort included journalists, doctors, lawyers, ministers, businesspersons, teachers, translators, farmers, and ranchers who successfully overcame formidable obstacles to emerge as distinguished and high-standing members of their respective societies. In segregated districts, merchants ran hotels, restaurants, barbershops, mom and pop mercantile stores, bakeries, tailor shops, labor agencies, taverns, laundries, and sundry other operations. Most of the professionals and businesspeople made only a passable life, yet their background, education, and success elevated them to a stratum higher than that of the struggling poor. On the other hand, some in their ranks amassed wealth and exerted influence even within mainstream society.[2]

Among such persons was Clara Brown, who earned recognition (from Colorado's exclusive, and all-white, circle of charter pioneers) for her business and philanthropic success. Born into slavery, she trekked toward Colorado a few years after her owners released her from bondage in 1857. North of the Denver area, she made do by taking whatever jobs availed themselves, but began to amass a respectable income from the earnings of local miners, doing their laundry and delivering their wives' babies. She invested her gains in real estate and mining claims while simultaneously lending out money and leasing her rental properties. She gained enormous respect and admiration from a cross-section of society for her financial and social achievements, but most prominently due to her good-heartedness: she donated to worthy causes, among them helping the needy and fledgling religious groups. Before she passed away in 1885, the Society of Colorado Pioneers invited Clara Brown to become one of its members. She was the first black and the first woman to be so honored, an acknowledgment indicating the acclaim bestowed upon those who had reached a high measure of success and made worthwhile contributions to frontier society.[3]

Doña Refugio Amador also knew wealth and received much respect for her accomplishments within Hispano society in New Mexico and even outside it. The wife of Martín Amador, a successful merchant who made his money as a U.S. government contractor during the early Territorial period, as owner of a freighting business during the 1870s, and as an investor in various other enterprises throughout his business career, Doña Refugio made her mark around Las Cruces as an exemplary administrator of her household (which consisted of several daughters and sons) and an astute overseer of her spouse's commercial affairs. Beginning in the 1860s, Doña Refugio tended to her husband's books, local business needs, and farming operations during Don Martín's frequent absences, managing their investments with acknowledged competence. When she passed away in 1907, she left a legacy as an undeniable business success story as well as having been a gracious and genteel lady, a kind mother, and a fine role model to her own middle-class children.[4]

Less respected (mainly because of her vocation), yet no less an achiever, was a Chinese woman in Nevada known to history only as "Mary." Apparently Mary had arrived in Virginia City's Chinatown in the early 1860s, established herself as a madam, and situated her house of prostitution at an accessible location next to a Chinese saloon. Her customers (of all races) generally would visit her business while patronizing the barroom, and in this fortuitous manner did Mary claim her own version of success in the West and come to constitute an element within the frontier "elite."[5]

Not much may be gathered from the record about the attitudes these three representatives of the well-off held about their own social standing. Certainly some who considered themselves of high standing imputed a modicum of importance to their type, as can be deduced by their comportment and public behavior. In San Francisco (and for that matter, other centers of black concentration such as Topeka) during and after the 1870s, the well-to-do segments of the African American community felt that social divisions within black communities ought to be acknowledged (in their eyes, the lower class represented a crude, unambitious, even violent segment).[6] These achievers valued education, feeling that formal training and learning refined the qualities befitting gentlemen and ladies.

To meet their needs as people of fine tastes and satisfy their desire to be with others of the same social rank and cultural refinement, they formed exclusive social circles composed of the better crust. Participation in these clubs required presenting themselves in the best fashion, holding fine banquets, and behaving as people of "high culture." Elites in San Francisco established literary clubs wherein they read and discussed the European classics. They attended art exhibits or lectures that had relevance to their lives as African Americans, or went to the opera or attended the several concerts that were part of San Francisco's black American life.[7]

Folks with the proper social graces also made efforts to minimize their Africanness. They might stress their white ancestry (in the belief that whiter skin elevated them above the common African American), point to their physical appearance, or make it a point to educate the wider public about the different racial components from which African Americans in the New World descended. For them, a person's worthiness in society (that is, white society) ought to be measured by demeanor, not by color. For the well-to-do, duty also called for women to be supportive of the kind of protocol expected of their male counterparts. For instance, balls and social events became the occasion for high-class African American women in San Francisco to flaunt their wealth, their cultured upbringing, and their fashions. They wore elaborate dresses and gowns to formal festivities and used the opportunity to showcase their jewels.[8]

Similarly did the Mexican American middle class regard itself as better than the rank and file. These elites held certain attitudes toward commoners, rejecting the larger mestizo population that daily performed work for them, believing their underlings to be uncultured plain folks with whom they should not mix publicly. Those with means enrolled their children in private schools (where present). They organized musical groups, dance societies, or literary clubs. In Tucson, where this select element remained rather strong well past the 1880s, many were well-schooled, quite religious, and overly confident of their moral standards.[9] Some members of this class took on airs of being cultured Mexicans, "Spaniards," or at least guardians of a "civilized" way of life, and by so doing, distanced themselves from the less fortune Mexicanos.

Guadalupe Vallejo projected such an image, at least as a manner of maneuvering around the racial frontier. Guadalupe descended from old Californio landowners and was the niece of Mariano Guadalupe Vallejo, a prominent pre-1846 military general and political leader. From a story she published in 1890 in *Century Magazine* titled "Ranch and Mission Days in Alta California," historians have deduced that she typified the erstwhile Californio power brokers who longed for the halcyon days of pre-1848 California when "Spaniards" lorded over the California ranchos. Given this group's declining stature in the last decades of the nineteenth century, members of the old gentility purportedly passed themselves off as "white" or "Spaniard," denigrating things associated with the Mexican lower class that Anglos associated with degeneracy.

But Guadalupe's literary pieces might well be misinterpreted by modern writers whose outlook extols the Mexican/American Indian heritage. From what is known about her private life, Guadalupe, like many others of her standing, was not adamant about claiming a Castilian heritage nor in renouncing her Mexican American identity. Further, she privately harbored resentment of mainstream white society. Like the Tucsonenses mentioned above, Guadalupe believed her language, culture, and religion to be superior to those of Anglos.

The haughty attitudes Mexican Americans and other colored elites displayed toward their own, thus, were long-standing customs of class instead of a self acclaimed racial superiority vis-à-vis the masses of Mexicanos. Publicly Guadalupe and those of her rank may have proclaimed themselves "Spanish" and even expressed a distaste for the uneducated poor, but within their own environs most did not renounce their cultural ties to *"lo mexicano."* Feigning whiteness served them in the effort to gain possible protection of their material holdings or in maintaining their social achievements.[10] Assuming two personas was the clever way by which people of color (as others have done elsewhere) steered around racial borders whenever they interfaced on the multicultural frontier.

Vallejo's role-playing illustrates more than the lingering inclination people had to consider lower-class people disapprovingly, and more than the ability of women to cross and recross racial partitions. It also indicates women's ability to traverse gender lines successfully, for example, by infiltrating some of the more exclusive male-dominated professions, in her case the intellectual world of publishing. Many more women than Vallejo prevailed in mostly male enterprises, and their triumphs gave new definitions to the roles generally ascribed to women. Such independent individuals, by their confidence and assertiveness, furthermore reconfigured social relations in the West. The grip men held over the business sector was upset, as women's control over a particular concern empowered them. Such control permitted women the luxury of making decisions affecting the family commercial establishment, their children's education, or, as in the case of Clara Brown's philanthropy, their community.

Like customs dictating recognition of class differences, so did conventions apropos to the family mirror those that pioneers had formerly observed in the homeland. People tended to subscribe to old family patterns, structural arrangements, relationships among parents and siblings, and time-honored gender duties. Yet no immutable features may be attributed to families in the West, as people tended to adjust to the reality of the new setting and in so doing discarded fragments of their home-grown culture. Nonetheless, historians have been able to describe some of these family units in general terms. Historian Juan Gómez-Quiñones, for instance, explains some of the decorum at the center of the Mexican American family:

> The principle values and social practices were those that upheld group order and harmony. Propriety *(formalidad)*, honesty in personal relations, and dedication to work were stressed. Elders enjoyed respect and were obeyed. Sons did not wear hats, smoke, or sit down in the presence of elders. Emphasis was placed on mutual respect in personal relations. Children were expected to kiss their parents' hands, stand when greeting adults, and remain standing when delivering an object until the recipient was finished with it. Long-term family friendships and supportive relations persisted, and formal visits were made by one family to another. During mourning periods the women in the family of the deceased wore black for six

months to a year. Orphaned children were adopted by relatives, godparents, childless couples, and spinsters.[11]

By contrast, the Chinese never entirely observed the social tenets that governed their own family structure back home, namely because the Chinese "family" in the West lacked all of its components. In households surveyed through the West, census takers typically found several men sharing a small room or tent, or perhaps living in boarding houses (many men reasoned it useless to buy property given their transient status). Yet even these ubiquitous bachelor arrangements displayed a semblance of family cohesion, as occupants improvised at establishing fraternal order. Within those confines, for instance, there lived ones to whom tenants might turn for empathy, moral support, understanding, and friendly discussion. They might inquire about adjustment strategies, such as asking for advice on how to mail money to loved ones in the homeland (a duty many of the Chinese workers considered obligatory).[12]

These units, as witnessed by contemporaries, were not improvised because Chinese men wanted to jettison their honored family structure, but rather because, until the end of the century, Chinese women were not part of the migration into the United States. Several reasons explain why Chinese wives and daughters did not accompany men west. For one thing, Chinese law prohibited the emigration of Chinese (either men or women) until the 1860s.[13] Also, the expense of financing the overseas journey deterred more than one person in the family from attempting the journey, and tradition in China furthermore discouraged wives from going abroad with their husbands. Then, frontier life in the new land was challenging for anyone, and male Chinese society did not feel that women were up to the task. Lastly, legislation was passed in the United States at the local, state, and national levels designed to curb the importation of Chinese prostitutes; these laws had the effect of deterring the immigration of all women.[14] Statistics reveal that in 1880 only 8,800 women had emigrated to the United States; this number accounted for only 5 percent of the entire Chinese population in the country.[15] As of 1890, the total population of Chinese women in the United States stood at about 3,800; deaths, return to the homeland, and other factors explain this decline.[16] As of 1890,

Chinese men outnumbered women twenty-seven to one,[17] an astonishing ratio even for a setting known for gender disparities.

Such a skewed ratio made it difficult for nuclear families to be the norm within Chinese communities. In any case, nuclear families were not the standard back in the homeland. In China, most poor people lived in a conjugal arrangement (husband and wife, the children, and the siblings of the man). The few fortunate to earn fair incomes lived in "stem" arrangements, wherein a son, along with his family, resided in the same household as that of his parents and their children. The wealthier classes preferred a "joint family" (it consisted of parents and their offspring, as well as the families of brothers of the husband, and the families of sons and grandsons), for together they could share and participate in the unit's financial holdings and interests. In the above family types, the male head of the household presided over an arrangement whose intent was to have children give emotional and material support to parents and related elders.[18]

Within these structures, and indeed in Chinese civilization, gender distinctions were scrupulously observed. Women faced serious disadvantages, for Chinese culture was male-dominant and extended limited privileges to women. Within the family unit, women amounted to subservient beings and were subject to the whims of the males. Upon marriage, a woman joined her husband's family, and was now to obey her spouse and care for his parents as they aged (as a widow, she followed the wishes of her eldest son). A woman's place was strictly in the home; rarely did women venture beyond their immediate village.[19]

While the homeland tradition of "bound feet" (the custom of restricting women to the home by binding their feet, thereby preventing the feet's growth and restricting women's wanderings) was not observed in the West, Chinese male society still confined women to the home and still insisted upon female subservience to men. Like other cultures in the United States, Chinese men expected women to be homebound, do the laundry and cooking, care for the family, and look the other way regarding male morality. Such customs were not too difficult to enforce in the U.S. West for a number of reasons. Chinese wives were reluctant to venture out in an unfamiliar environment, could rarely afford to leave the house due to poverty, and were seldom exposed to socializing agencies in the West that might "liberate" them.[20]

Lamentably, a disproportionate number of Chinese women living in the West (compared to their Mexican and African American counterparts) were prostitutes; one source puts the estimate for 1880 in San Francisco at 50 percent.[21] The phenomenon had appeared during the first stages of Chinese immigration and remained as time progressed (the percentage did drop over time); women prostitutes, in fact, became a more valuable commodity following the Chinese Exclusion Act in 1882. Few women were willing participants in the practice. Mostly from the peasant class, many came as kidnap victims, others under the illusion that they were coming to Gold Mountain as picture brides or to earn a better livelihood, while still others were bought from destitute families in China. Upon arriving in the United States, the unsuspecting women were acquired by men wanting them for personal use or by those engaged in immoral commerce. As a consequence, many women found themselves relegated to cribs or brothels that were often controlled by secret societies.[22]

From the custom of female domination in China, such women fell into another trap of despotism. On the U.S. frontier, they had no more social freedoms than in the homeland. While elements in Chinese society (both in the homeland and in the U.S. West) may have possessed notions of prostitutes as stained with immorality, for many the practice of selling one's body did not fall outside the context of sexist customs. In the view of a predominantly male Chinese community, prostitutes served as revenue generators for those who owned or managed them, or as property to please men of all races if called upon to do so.[23]

Nonetheless, prostitutes devised ways to counter the suffocating oppression of their lives. Some stole from their clients, took personal complaints to the courts, or turned to local social groups wanting to curb immorality.[24] In fact, cases of Chinese women successfully establishing their own profitable business in the trade do exist. The most prominent example is probably that of Ah Toy, who arrived in San Francisco in 1849, already with an agenda for success and the assets to carry it out. She was youthful, attractively built, bilingual (English and her native tongue), and, unlike the case with so many of her gender, beholden to no one for her services. Soon, Ah Toy began work out of her own premises, but her list of customers grew so abundantly that she employed two other women to meet demand. This arrangement itself proved unwieldy after a time, so that Ah Toy perforce relocated to more comfortable quarters. By 1852, Ah Toy managed two brothels and, according to some reports, had even established branches in Sacramento and elsewhere in Northern California. Her net worth is unknown though apparently it afforded her a comfortable lifestyle.

Ah Toy's decline as a madam occurred within a few years of her arrival in San Francisco. She had constant brushes with the law, but more ominously, with fellow countrymen running rings of organized prostitution who wished to eliminate her competition. By 1857, she had closed down her enterprise and thereafter found making a livelihood in the West by other means a difficult one. Her career as a madam, however, had for a moment defied the customs of her homeland and perhaps those of the trans-Mississippi West.

Ah Toy merits mention not solely because she succeeded financially (albeit only fleetingly), but because she represented the manner by which women in the West ably treaded the gender frontier. First, she had made her way to Gold Mountain in violation of societal and male-ordained norms that dissuaded (and in her case forbade) single women from leaving their home territory. In her particular trade, furthermore, she successfully manipulated men, for Chinese prostitutes (their powerlessness notwithstanding) could— in their own gender sphere—control their lives by, say, bargaining with customers for price or rejecting their business by feigning illness. Ah Toy restructured labor relations, moreover, not solely because she competed with her Chinese male counterparts, but also because she enticed and manipulated men regardless of political or economic influence. Indeed, her customers included all races, many of them willing to violate norms regarding the color divide. Intimate contact could most definitely occur despite taboos, and was the most private manner by which Westerners compromised their prejudices on the racial frontier.[25]

But not even the intimate frontier converted patrons into admirers of each other's customs. Least interested in the empowerment of coexisting cultures were whites, who of all the races meeting in the West had the power to dominate the competition in every way possible. Blatantly and otherwise, the majority society deprecated "foreign" communities. They condemned males of color as too domineering and women as inclined to immorality. Stereotypically, one commentator in California during the 1850s disparaged both Chinese and African American women (and probably thought the same of Mexican women), declaring: "Unlike the Oriental nations, the Chinese have sent hither swarms of their females, a large part of whom are a depraved class; and though with complexions in some instance approaching fair, their whole physiognomy indicates but a slight removal from the African race."[26]

Actually, condemnation of minority group institutions and customs was often expressed but did not become a political issue. But why would mainstream society, which did not hesitate to smother political or economic resistance from minorities, not try to crush the customs of racial minorities? For one thing, minorities were not socially a bothersome lot. Segregation, as was intended, acted to minimize contact among the several players on the racial frontier; what was not visible need not be squelched! Minority groups, furthermore, did not ordinarily seek integration into the social realm of Anglo American life as they did entrance into the economic and political systems. Africans, Chinese, and Mexicans simply showed little inclination to disturb the social fabric of the white West by, say, openly courting white women or pursuing intermarriage. In fact, a romantic overture misread by a white woman could well plunge a man of color into a quagmire. In Fort Washakie, Wyoming, in 1887, a buffalo soldier by the name of James Glass responded to what he believed was consent by a washerwoman named Mary Snell for a sexual tryst. When the white woman rebuffed him, Glass apologized for the affront, but to no avail. Her complaints to fort authorities produced a dishonorable discharge and a five-year penitentiary sentence (later revoked) for Glass.[27] Understanding such mores and ancillary social norms, people of color maintained a safe distance from unpleasant or potentially disastrous contact.

Additionally, minorities probably were content to be loyal to their own subculture and saw no compelling reason to contest white social institutions in the same way they challenged Anglo Americans on the economic and political fronts. In-group customs might also have worked to the advantage of those at the top; class conflicts within minority communities produced, perhaps as desired, social divisions allowing Anglos to maintain continued domination. A last explanation for lack of interest in what took place inside African American districts, Chihuahuitas, or Chinatowns was the aforementioned tolerance that accompanied frontier living. People, regardless of color, needed to work together for the common goal of survival. If the customs that people practiced in the relative privacy of their homes and segregated quarters did not violate public policy, why let them become an issue of contention? When cultural practices—cockfighting or gambling, for instance— violated laws, officials did step in.

Thus, the expectations that minorities entertained about perpetuating time-honored customs faced little resistance from those who otherwise oppressed them politically and economically. But familiar ways of life also persisted for a bevy of other reasons. Certainly, the frontier offered little chance for acculturation through osmosis—unwritten doctrines or strictures impeded opportunities for whites and people of color to mix in schools, the churches, or other public settings. Anglo American settlers in the West, furthermore, did not even bother about the Americanization of Africans, Chinese, and Mexicans. A few church groups, to be sure, did take on such initiatives, as in the case of rescue homes managed by white missionary women in San Francisco; they sought to rehabilitate Chinese prostitutes by submerging them in programs steeped in white middle-class values and Christian teachings. Among those saved was Chy Hay, who according to Methodist officials never forgot her stay at their mission home during the 1870s. Though she married a "heathen" man after having left the Methodist home, she herself accepted Christianity. In reality, most of the prostitutes who found solace in these types of missions refused acculturation, preferring loyalty to the customs of their upbringing.[28]

While the preference was for old ways, the social environment on the racial frontier nonetheless caused change. The frontier obliged people of color to modify customs such as those applicable to women's responsibilities. Women's assumption of male tasks on the frontier (such as fighting Indians or doing traditional men's chores around the home or farms) weakened the general belief that women should subscribe unhesitatingly to the principles of domesticity. Consequently, women's roles took directions deviating from proscriptions common in the homeland. In the West, necessity overpowered tradition, and women augmented their responsibilities when they supplemented a husband's or father's salary. Chinese wives, among others, began coupling their duties by doing outside work at home (as seamstresses or washerwomen) or taking in boarders.[29] Such burdens evoked among the Chinese women ideas of independence, or self-sufficiency. Others physically left their home to work as dressmakers, laundresses, or unskilled laborers. As they dared do so, Chinese women could not help but experience empowerment, if not a liberating sense of accomplishment upon repudiating the will of males.

Other conditions in the West further liberalized the lives of Chinese women. Marriages, which increased by the 1880s (both in the big cities such as San Francisco or Los Angeles and in remote settlements, like those in Idaho) diluted customs. Those who married could expect their former life to be overlooked, as in Chinese American communities in which prostitution was seen as an avenue of survival and not a voluntary career undertaken by the debauched. The married state meant Chinese women no longer had to be homebound; indeed, it compelled women to assume the responsibility of assisting the husband and family in carrying out frontier chores.[30] The general rate of marriage increases owed much to legislation designed to control prostitution (which had the aftereffect of allowing former prostitutes to marry); the Chinese Exclusion Act, which permitted the immigration of wives married to members of the merchant class; and the work of missionaries wanting to rescue Chinese women from a life of vice.[31]

Indeed, Chinese marriages in San Francisco and elsewhere by the latter decades of the nineteenth century started resembling the traditional nuclear family in which men left for work in the morning, leaving women to preside over domestic affairs. Household arrangements also departed from the custom in China as mothers-in-law no longer intervened, as wives amassed status given the dearth of women available for marriage in the West, and as men gained greater respect for mates who could supplement their income and enhance their prestige as economic achievers. Women's own self-esteem increased in these evolving circumstances, which augmented their voice as family partners. The changing role of the Chinese American wife naturally had implications for the entire household unit. Children from these marriages saw parents in a different light than did their counterparts in the homeland. Old Chinese customs weakened simultaneously for the offspring, as more of them came to identify with the country of their birth. Increasingly, Chinese families committed themselves to living in the West and adopting desirable U.S. customs.[32]

Change in the traditional family also involved exogamy, though intermarriage never became so extensive that it alarmed white society or threatened the family structure of any of the participating groups. One such case involved Polly and Charlie Bemis, who broke cultural scriptures in early Idaho by exchanging wedding vows, then living as man and wife for several decades. During the 1860s, Chinese camps had formed in Idaho as a result of gold discoveries; by 1870, the Chinese constituted 26 percent of the total population in the territory and 58.6 percent of those who reported their occupation as miners (in contrast, the Chinese female population numbered slightly more than 100, or 3.0 percent of the total Chinese population).

Polly had arrived in Idaho from China as an eighteen-year-old in 1870, the property (prostitute) of a fellow countryman apparently doing well locally as a labor agent. She met Charlie, her future spouse, when she nursed the miner back to health on the order of her owner; Charlie suffered from injuries inflicted upon him in what appeared a personal brawl. In the course of Charlie's rehabilitation, the two fell in love and subsequently married.

Polly Bemis apparently lived as coequal with her husband and thus broke not only from the arbitrary control of her immediate owner but from the dictates of the customs she had known in her homeland. Change came to her in ways not possible in the makeup or the tradition of the Chinese family. She worked the couple's land cooperatively, raising farm animals and growing shrubs and flowers in her personal garden. Change also occurred in that the local white community bestowed a generous amount of respect upon Polly Bemis. Personal attributes contributed to that recognition: she was possessed of an agreeable disposition and congenial personality, and took delight in playing host to travelers passing through the Bemis's small ranch. Over the years, her generosity became legendary, so that today her story is a mix of fact and myth. But there is no doubt that a Chinese American woman married to a white man named Charlie Bemis lived in Warren, Idaho, until death separated them (she died in 1932) and that an old way of life could certainly take a different turn on the trans-Mississippi frontier.[33]

The more common cases of exogamy involved Mexican females. Of women from the several races crossing paths on the frontier, Mexicans were most likely to skirt custom by marrying outside their in-group. Spanish/Mexican society before 1848 had been accepting of marriage among different racial groups (for example, Indians and Africans), and such tolerance persisted into the postwar period as women entered into cross-cultural arrangements with Anglo men. Many times, however, such unions involved daughters of the well-to-do. The reasons for such Anglo male/Mexican female unions were varied: they entailed love, the desire to improve economic status, the loosening of restrictions upon Mexican women, sexual disparities in the West (not enough white women for Anglo men), and so forth.[34] While these factors account for some interracial unions, more selfish reasons also entered into the formula. Mexican landowners or businessmen desired their daughter to marry an Anglo (in some cases, they arranged such marriages) to see that the family formed an alliance that might help it in white society. The strategy was also intended to insure that one's pre-1848 status continued. Mergers also assisted the Mexican elite in developing relations with those more closely connected to the frontier economy.[35]

When Mexicanas married outside their culture and community, they still practiced Catholicism and abided by such Mexican observances as having *padrinos* (godparents) for their children. But they parted from custom by managing their homes according to the wishes of their Anglo spouse, learning English, and dispatching their progeny to American schools.[36] They also played a hand in defining the new identity of their offspring. Studies do not yet exist as to the cultural thoroughfares such offspring took, though fragmentary evidence indicates that some (as is the case today) became completely absorbed into Anglo life while others entered Mexican American society with only their English names distinguishing them from the rest. No doubt, however, the children of interracial unions had to forge their own pathway along the sensitive racial crossroads intersecting the color frontier.

When women decided it was necessary to help with the family budget (or determined to earn their own wages) by joining the labor pool, agreed to assume responsibilities other than keeping house, or opted to marry outside their in-group, they successfully made strides in the perpetual tug of war against the custom that they ought to be faithful to tradition and deferential to male mandates. On occasion, such power plays turned custom upside down. In the year 1868, for instance, one Louise Fly appeared before court in Gonzales County, Texas, accused of abusing her husband, David. Louise defended herself from the allegations by declaring that David was a ne'er-do-well whom she did not love anyway. David wished help from the court in that he had suffered mental anguish, physical mistreatment, and punishment from his wife's refusal to have intimate relations with him. Louise maintained her feisty disposition before the judge by further conceding that she preferred white men (both were African American). Louise and David ultimately reached some kind of amicable pact, for the census of 1870 showed them living as man and wife with two children.[37]

In the everyday life of the frontier, of course, the inroads made into the world of male dominance rarely stretched to the degree that Louise Fly supposedly took them. Certainly, patriarchy was brought into question in many relationships and hierarchy rethought in others. Women also may have found power in marrying Anglo men; if the spouse commanded political and economic influence, certainly wives and their children were all the better off for it. In the end, however, racial communities existed almost as transplants of their counterparts in the homeland—maintaining customs surrounding class distinctions, ideas about family and women, and so on. People in the segregated enclaves adopted some Anglo American ways, but seldom did they renounce their heritage or disguise themselves as anything but the group of their upbringing, as was the case with Guadalupe Vallejo. As such, they made the Western frontier a diverse region, much different from the one early historians portrayed.

CHAPTER 5

Identities

The great majority, however, carried to their new homes a firm desire to transfer to the West the cultural institutions of the East. They came determined to make no compromise with the environment; they would plant a civilization complete with schools, churches, literary societies, newspapers, libraries, and a thriving cultural life.

—RAY ALLEN BILLINGTON, America's Frontier Heritage

The noted historian who penned these oft-quoted words in 1974 obviously had in mind no other than white frontier people. He wrote, after all, at a time before mainstream historians had been sensitized to the deeds of different races and ethnic groups out West. Like white folks, people of color also clung pertinaciously to a homeland identity. They trusted the merit of their beliefs, cultural habits, intellectual record, and aesthetic forms. Because they thought in such a way, diverse types of identities intersected in the West, none of them conceding total acculturation.

The frontier, therefore, became a setting wherein racial identity and culture were associate factors in the competition for survival. Their presence stoked ethnocentric sentiments and heightened tension over ways of worshiping, educational curricula, racial ideology, secular/religious celebrations, and folk beliefs. Negatively, cultural chauvinism begot contempt, and sometimes violent retribution against the opposition. Positively, cultural identity acted as a force of empowerment, as it encouraged the different players to extol their own virtues and challenge others who considered themselves better.

People of different races jostled daily on the job and skirmished on the political front, but they spent the longer span of their lives in segregated social environments marked by distinct and specific traditions, conventions, customs, and even mindsets. In these pockets of cultural homogeneity, people of color made adjustments essential for success within mainstream society, but they nonetheless maintained an affinity for the old. Nowhere else but in Chinese settlements, for example, were "joss houses" (from *deos,* the Portuguese word for god; the Portuguese had used them in China). Such religious places, which had surfaced in San Francisco by the 1850s and in remote places such as Idaho and Nevada by the 1860s and 1870s, respectively, were usually no more than ordinary structures where those wishing to meditate housed idols and other religious paraphernalia. In these sanctuaries, none but the Chinese could find consolation, divine inspiration, and confirmation of a specific faith.[1] Whether by design or preference, racial/ethnic enclaves fulfilled people's conception of the frontier as a place for implanting their own cultural accoutrements and exercising group identity.

Frontier circumstances permitted people of varying cultural backgrounds to affirm their devotion to standing theological beliefs, for instance. Naturally, religious sects of many sorts took root in the trans-Mississippi region, each serving to nurture and sustain the identity of its adherents and believers. Mexicans found a common attachment to Catholicism (the only major group in the West to do so), though their commitment varied from uncontested devotion to skepticism. Priests ministering to Mexicans tended to be foreigners (Europeans) who did not understand the ways of their flock. Mexican Americans and newly arrived immigrants nonetheless remained true to the Catholicism of their forbears, helping to build churches where needed, assisting priests (when present) to carry on their duties, and observing holy days in the Catholic calendar.[2]

Since the Spanish colonial era, however, Mexicans had drifted into a popular religiosity that met immediate needs. No one in the mid-nineteenth century typified this brand of faith more than Antonio José Martínez, the "*cura* of Taos." Born and raised in New Mexico, he had early displayed a penchant for education and, by a regimen of self-learning, had eventually made his way to the seminary in Durango, from which he received his ordination into the priesthood in 1822. From the 1830s until he died in 1867, he served as the priest of Taos, establishing there a school for young people and disseminating lessons from books that he published himself. During the Mexican era, he had demanded that the church eliminate the fees charged by priests to perform the sacraments, argued for greater autonomy among local parishes, and, at least according to his critics, violated his vows of celibacy.

In the 1850s, he carried on an open schism with Bishop Jean Baptiste Lamy of Santa Fe over theological issues, tithing, politicking, and what Martínez and his parishioners felt to be the arrogance of foreign priests, as well as over the bishop's ethnocentric views toward the natives. Lamy threatened Martínez with excommunication if he did not cease his insolence and indiscretions. But Martínez rallied those loyal to him in Taos, and a tumult between the forces of the two principals seemed possible. When Lamy carried out his threat in June 1857, the result was the appearance of two churches in Taos: an unofficial one loyal to Martínez, the other recognized by Lamy. Martínez's followers in Taos and elsewhere included Catholics who supported his defense of local traditions and other *nuevo mexicanos* who resented new clergymen questioning generations-old spiritual traditions and deriding native customs. The defrocked Martínez continued until his death to work among the community of "faithful" in Taos, conducting services and administering the sacraments in his own sanctuary. Lamy simply ignored him.[3]

The paradox of the West as both an intolerant and tolerant setting also allowed pioneers to utilize education as an apparatus for upholding and inculcating homeland identities. As a rule, most community leaders like Martínez entertained a thirst for learning and broadening knowledge. As the Reverend John T. Jenifer of Virginia City, Nevada, informed readers about African Americans in 1865 through one of the black San Francisco newspapers: "If our people ever are to be raised from the dust into which they have been crushed and ground for two hundred and forty-five years, it is to be done by that potent lever, education, and especially among our youths."[4]

Among those who heeded such advice were the black soldiers of the Twenty-fifth Infantry, one of the all-black units Congress organized in 1869. Like so many African Americans, they viewed schooling as a path to equality and upward mobility. Most of them illiterate to the point of not being able to write their names, they voluntarily took army-sponsored classes (taught by chaplains), and with time several acquired good reading and writing skills. Of their enthusiasm for and understanding of the value of schooling, a chaplain at Fort Davis, Texas, noted in 1877:

> The ambition to be all that soldiers should be is not confined to a few of these sons of an unfortunate race. They are possessed of the notion that the colored people of the whole country are more or less affected by their conduct in the army. The chaplain is sometimes touched by evidence of their manly anxiety to be well thought of at Army HQ and throughout the states. This is the bottom secret of their patient toil, and surprising progress in the effort to get at least an elementary education.[5]

Yet those responsible for providing fundamental education to "unfortunate races" in the West were not always so willing to extend such amenities. Tension resulted as disadvantaged communities demanded concessions such as integration into public school systems, believing their commitment to an extended stay in the United States and a loyalty to U.S. life entitled them to formal enlightenment. Rebuffed, their alternative was self-improvement. African Americans, like other minorities, attempted the establishment of parallel agencies of instruction to act as surrogates for mainstream institutions.

In segregated districts such enterprises fell to the superintendence of literate members of the community. These persons might volunteer their services, then make do with whatever books, supplies, and equipment might be mustered up to help the student body.[6] Where possible, residents of the black community financed schools that facilitated advanced learning. In Morris County, Kansas, concerned citizens, through great sacrifice, established the Colored Academy in 1881. This institution required an entrance exam in basic knowledge, charged tuition, and had as its purpose getting students to acquire the necessary preparation so that they might attend the state university.[7]

While it is difficult to determine what kind of emphasis such private schools placed on racial uniqueness, it would seem logical that in addition to the core curriculum, mentors referenced a positive historical record, pointed to special heroes and their contributions to world civilization, or in other ways reinforced in-group esteem. Away from the oversight of those who protected the status quo, group identity tended to be nurtured and hardly disturbed. Impressionable youngsters could hardly avoid getting a psychological and emotional boost, ironically, by being kept apart on the racial frontier.

The West as an imagined place for free expression, yet one segregated along racial lines, encouraged "ethnic/race" artistic display. Through literary forms or dramatic performances, educated or semieducated folks who were concentrated in segregated quarters waged a resistance struggle against any type of cultural disparagement while self-assuredly expounding on the glory that shaped their individual and collective being. Published literature never reached a circulation that in and of itself strengthened minority group identity in the nineteenth century (such a function fell to folklore). That dearth of published works may be attributed to the general illiteracy of the population, the lack of wider demand for race/ethnic stories, and a general bias on the part of publishers against handling the works of a subordinated class.[8] But people of color did write! There were, for example, Mexican Americans who authored autobiographies or left memoirs for personal reasons, such as revising the characterization given to them by others, namely Anglo Americans (the most literate of all the races out West), or plainly correcting biased interpretations presented by Anglo chroniclers/historians of the era. Juan N. Seguín of Texas, for example, wrote his memoirs (ca. 1850s) in hopes of gaining exoneration from accusations that he was a traitor to the Republic of Texas. José Antonio Navarro, another Tejano, wrote his *Apuntes Históricos Interesantes de San Antonio de Béxar,* also during the 1850s, in an attempt to overturn what he perceived as plainly disparaging portrayals of the Spanish and Mexican past in Texas history.[9]

Then there were the narrators of what are called *testimonios* (testimonials). Done during the 1870s at the prompting of Hubert Howe Bancroft, dubbed the "Historian of the West," these testimonials (defined as "elicited dictations" of recollections because many were dictated to Bancroft's agents) by old Californio settlers remain in unpublished manuscript form at the Bancroft Library at the University of California at Berkeley. What marks these recollections is an intention similar to Navarro's: they offer a counterhistory to that recorded by mainstream society in the West, and illustrate something of the identity the Californios held of themselves as a community in the several decades following the conquest.[10] These testimonios reveal a variety of sentiments, among them a resentment toward Anglo Americans, a desire to make a successful adjustment to U.S. life, and an appeal to mainstream society for racial and economic parity.

Among the most powerful of the testimonios was the monumental account dictated to Bancroft's agent by Mariano Guadalupe Vallejo. In Mexican California, Don Mariano had ranked among the state's wealthiest landowners; once he realized the futility of fighting against the Anglo invaders in 1846, he had acquiesced to the new regime, hoping American rule would be an improvement over Mexican sovereignty. But he had erred in his calculation; by the 1860s he had lost huge portions of his estate to American squatters and faced further impoverishment from having to defend his holdings in the courts. Understandably, he was bitter in 1875 when he gave his testimonio, and both subtly and boldly accused white settlers of being unjust, deceitful, cruel, and corrupt. He singled out Anglo lawyers and the U.S. courts as duplicitous and held them responsible for his misfortunes. Vallejo and other informants simultaneously attempted to revise old stereotypes that had taken form as cultures clashed in the West. Many took umbrage at the skewed manner by which whites assumed that they alone had "tamed" the frontier.[11]

More public displays of resistance to racial characterizations and reaffirmation of self-identity were evident in the stories and/or editorials regularly published in newspapers owned or operated by people of color. By nature, such newspapers were located in urban areas of the West with high concentrations of minority populations. In the case of African Americans, the best-known newspapers were published in California (*The Mirror of the Times,* the *Pacific Appeal,* and the *Elevator* all served San Francisco from about 1856 to 1862, 1862 to 1882, and 1865 to the 1890s, respectively) and Kansas (*Colored Citizen,* 1878, and the *American Citizen,* 1888), both in Topeka.[12]

Editors viewed their role as extending beyond routine reporting of news. So far as African American journalists were concerned, the press spoke for blacks who had few other vehicles for protest. Among the things editors did, therefore, was to remind readers (including whites, one presumes) of the principles upon which American democracy rested. They also addressed such topics as equality and the need to look forward despite obstacles; they devoted much space to encouraging race achievement and publicizing success stories.[13]

The most famous black journalists included William L. Eagleson, the editor of Topeka's *Colored Citizen,* and Peter Anderson and Philip A. Bell, both of San Francisco's *Pacific Appeal,* though Bell became better associated with the *Elevator,* which incidentally could boast of being the longest running black newspaper in the United States up to that time. As editor, Bell (who received his education at the African Free School in New York) won renown for his attention to black politics, his coverage of race friction, his extensive chronicling of black activities, and his insistence that blacks form self-help clubs designed to agitate for equality. When he died in 1889, his colleagues proclaimed him to be the "Napoleon of the West." Anderson, on the other hand, rejected the idea of launching segregated societies; to do so was to acquiesce in segregation. Instead, he believed that African Americans should strive for equality as individuals and as Americans, just like white people.[14]

Minority actors and public performers might not have had the consciousness of journalists such as Philip A. Bell, but they nonetheless contributed to community empowerment by furthering social identity. Invariably entertaining audiences of their own race or ethnicity in segregated quarters, theatrical players enjoyed the space and open consent to mock oppressors (be they Anglos or pretentious elites in their own community). They had the liberty to employ ethnic/race humor and sarcasm to achieve the same end. In carrying out such intentions, they could regale their audiences with in-group dialogue, the clever use of body language, or an acting style readily understandable to and appreciated by the spectators.

Mexicans, as a case in point, viewed (and desired) plays and dramas written in Spanish, if not playwrights from Spain or Mexico, and arranged by members of their own community. Popular or dramatic plays reaffirmed religious views or reprised people's finest historical achievements. In numerous Spanish-speaking communities, local citizens, church clubs, or family members held *pastorelas* (Christmas plays such as *Los Pastores*). Or they reenacted historical events, such as in the play *Los Tejanos,* which recounted the Texas invasion of New Mexico (and its subsequent failure) in 1841.[15]

A more formal theatre appeared in the larger cities of the West after the 1860s, as occurred in Los Angeles and San Antonio. Los Angeles was actually presenting dramas by the 1850s in four local theatres established by Californios or by Anglos who had been won over to Hispanic culture. A decade later, Los Angeles had become the site of even more theatrical houses and productions, joined by its rival to the north, the city of San Francisco. In Texas, the theatre came later than on the west coast and lacked the Golden State's sophistication: semiprofessionals ordinarily constituted the acting groups in San Antonio in the 1870s and 1880s. These cities as well as many other Southwestern towns (among them Tucson, Arizona, and Laredo, Texas) and ranching communities also came to be visited by itinerant acting troupes from Mexico after the Civil War. The relevance of the theatre to Mexican American communities in the West was such that during the 1860s some professional theatre companies fled the turmoil in Mexico for the safety of California, where they continued to offer a repertoire of plays.[16]

Theatre did not constitute the only genre of the performing arts to find expression among minority populations in the trans-Mississippi region. Music, too, in all its variances served to reinforce identity and foster community cohesiveness. Talented musicians and singers not only pleased audiences, but spoke to skill and natural ability that transcended race. Among accomplished artists in the West were African Americans Emma and Louise Hyers of Sacramento, California, who excelled in the performance of classical music. Similarly famous in California as classical musicians during the 1860s were African Americans Sarah Miles Taylor and William Blake. Communities with the ability to advance musical training helped when able to do so. By 1877, Sacramento was home to the Pacific Musical Association that sought to groom talented prospects in the tradition of classical music.[17]

More ubiquitously, of course, there existed the music of popular ensembles and that of more formally organized bands. In a frontier setting, the latter might well be called before mixed audiences, as certainly was the case with the all-black Twenty-fifth Infantry band. The group played in all kinds of settings: wherever they were stationed, the soldiers delighted fellow servicemen or community residents assembled at the military fort or in nearby towns. Invariably, the soldiers were recruited to be part of official military functions where music would enrich the event. In several areas of the West, local folks and communities asked them to participate in patriotic holidays or to provide the appropriate mood at funerals.[18]

An infinite number of popular and folk expressions—which complemented religion, education, literature, and the arts—also shaped and maintained identity on the frontier. Characteristic of life in segregated enclaves were numerous types of entertainment activities (both organized and improvised) and folk practices that helped those newly arrived from the homeland make the transition to the hinterlands, offered escape to those that faced hostility from outsiders, and soothed all still faithful to the mother culture. Popular and folk traditions further strengthened community-defined expectations, guided proper cultural behavior, and validated the worth of communities. They helped to fend off or struggle against greater forces, whether real or imagined. While engaging in fun and games, for instance, participants not only amused themselves, but could (perhaps, for example, in rodeo events) scoff at the alleged superiority of other peoples with whom they coexisted. Folk convictions also served people (generally uneducated) in explaining natural phenomena or interpreting life's complexities.

Both secular and religious festivals became occasions for buttressing a shared identity, as those engaged in the frivolity observed the achievements of the homeland and paid homage to familiar figures. At these times, communities might celebrate the birth or death of a national hero or commemorate a landmark event in their common heritage. Speeches praised the exploits of a noble patriot, a pivotal strike for freedom, or a movement for liberation. Those attending rejoiced in a glorious past as they milled about the festival grounds. National symbols and motifs abounded at these affairs, as people went "native," wearing the costumes of the homeland, eating indigenous foods, or delighting in their own music.

African Americans found several occasions for such festivities. In California before the Civil War—but also in other parts of the trans-Mississippi region—African American communities searching for an independence date (July 4 did not mean the same thing for them as it did for whites) set August 1 aside for merrymaking because it was recognized as emancipation day in the British West Indies. When celebrants observed August 1 in Denver, Colorado, in 1865, they participated in a parade that included carriages, buntings, music, orations, and good food. Much of the black community in the area attended.[19]

By 1864, however, the Emancipation Proclamation (announced in 1862) was emerging as a more proper "American" fete day to symbolize freedom from slavery. It was recognized that year in Leavenworth, Kansas, in Virginia City, Nevada, and in other parts of the West. The 1864 jubilee in Leavenworth reportedly attracted huge crowds, while ones held in Portland and other Oregon towns in the late 1860s featured important members of the black community giving keynote addresses that continued the themes of liberty and equality. In San Francisco, similarly, Emancipation Day called for glorifying the African past, and through singing, speeches, and pageantry, organizers and participants eulogized their ties to the African continent. Simultaneously, they held up as heroes slaves such as Denmark Vesey and Nat Turner.[20] As did African Americans throughout the United States, blacks in the West rejoiced over the Fifteenth Amendment, which states ratified on March 30, 1870.[21]

The commemoration of these kinds of "national holidays" did not manifest separatist tendencies among the revelers. In fact, such events became occasions where the different races found a common interest and cooperated for the sake of memorializing a cherished principle: freedom. Organizers might have to rely on other groups for the use of public space, materials, or incidentals such as wagons in order to complete arrangements and have a successful ceremony. Moreover, activities followed a pattern copied from parallel celebrations, as in the case of parades. The themes of speeches tended to be universal: black orators, as was the case above, spoke of humankind's love of freedom and opportunity, and the heroes they eulogized embodied universal values. Denmark Vesey and Nat Turner cherished liberty as much as Washington or Lincoln.

Religious festivals served functions similar to those of their secular counterparts, as people used the entertainment form to pay fealty to the homeland creed. Such festivals as were held throughout the West invited mass public demonstration of particular beliefs and permitted the faithful to renew their convictions. Participants found reaffirmation of their identity in familiar cultural symbols integrated into these memorials. National flags, edibles, and, in the case of the Chinese, pyrotechnics added to the frivolity of otherwise solemn events.

In the West, the Chinese observed a long list of religious holidays according to the Chinese lunar-year calendar, which essentially followed the agricultural cycle.[22] At the end of January or the start of February, Chinese Americans held the Lunar New Year Festival and commemorated it just as they had in China. This festival was first celebrated in California during the early 1850s, then became common by the 1860s, and could be found in other parts of the West, even in the Dakota Territory. Wherever the Chinese immigrants had settled, workers took time off to pay for debts and generally launch a fresh start for the year. They tidied up their houses and decorated their communities with such items as Chinese flags, exchanged presents, and celebrated by playing games of chance, setting off firecrackers (to scare off evil spirits), and consuming food, wine, rice whiskey, and the like.[23]

Second in significance to the above holiday was the Ch'ing Ming Festival (also called the Tomb Festival) held in April. This occasion also involved several days of ritual as people paid their respects to their dead kin. Chinese religious tradition mandated that individuals tend to the graves of deceased relatives lest the living displease the spirits and be reproached by fellow villagers. As in the homeland, therefore, the Chinese in the West cleaned cemetery plots, offered their dead kin food and money, and asked their ancestors to help those on earth. The revelry included parades, music, costumes, and firecrackers; the celebration intended to have both the living and the dead rejoice in communal gaiety.[24]

The Chinese clearly had much regard for family members who had passed on. Survivors took special care during funerals to insure that the departed were protected from the evil forces to which they were temporarily vulnerable. The celebration that accompanied funerals—which included elaborate processions to the burial plot, the firing of pyrotechnics, bands playing, and gongs sounding—was in part designed to protect the deceased from supernatural elements. At the cemetery, the personal belongings of the loved one were buried as well in order to allow the deceased to arrive as completely prepared as possible in the other world.[25]

People, then, generally found the appropriate means to resurrect traditional festival forms even when thousands of miles separated them from their primary culture. Identity consequently seldom broke down, for immigrants consciously strove to build communities based on the model they knew in the homeland. Preferred beliefs, common rituals, and a familiar creed culturally invested them, even as they otherwise encountered political or economic travail. In the West, they could more easily come to comprehend the order of the world or offer solace to loved ones through these means.

Individual modes of relaxation and entertainment suffered no major alteration either. Impersonal, less structured, and calmer modes of leisure provided continuity as people contented themselves with native sports, in-group contests, and traditional recreational games. Gambling, as a leisure activity, was especially dear and personal to many of the immigrants, as it was to the Chinese. Though many Westerners found gambling quaint, and even disgusting and repugnant, their abhorrence perplexed the Chinese, who considered hazarding an integral aspect of their heritage and even personality. Gambling, in fact, constituted part of the Chinese belief system: for many in the homeland, as well as for sojourners in the West, chance was a force to be dealt with in life. A person's (good) fortune could change with the stroke of luck: why not gamble on fate?[26]

Gambling, consequently, came in all forms and could be found in just about every Chinese quarter. In the isolated regions of the West—mining camps, railroad villages, or fledgling settlements such as those in Arizona or on the Rocky Mountain frontier—the Chinese took to gaming as much as other races or nationalities.[27] Games of risk embraced a wide spectrum—among them dominoes and dice—but the most popular ones were Fan-Tan and lottery. The former sport, played on a table, had as its object guessing the arbitrary number of cards (or objects such as beans, coins, or buttons), left at the bottom of a cup as the dealer withdrew four at a time. It remained, as had been the case in the homeland, a integral part of Chinese cultural life, ranking among the most widespread of free-time revelries in the larger cities like Los Angeles and San Francisco.[28] Almost as popular as Fan-Tan was Pok Kop Piu, or lottery. To participate in this game, the public simply bought a ticket, either at a designated place or from a lottery agent, and took a chance at winning the drawing. Most visible in California Chinatowns, it made its way as an entertainment routine into the hinterlands of Idaho and of other interior states.[29]

Anathema (and illegal) to puritanical frontiersmen, gambling thus fulfilled the passions of those who saw betting and wagering as a cultural tenet. For devotees, it not only imbued them with personal gratification, but culturally uplifted them. On the frontier, gambling lingered alongside a long list of "odd" cultural elements that gave orderliness and cohesiveness to diverse types of communities, all with the instinct for human survival.

Common also to frontier communities was folklore. As did festivals, celebrations, and gambling, folklore revealed itself on the frontier in unique variants. It was present in different languages. It interpreted a variety of experiences. But it was common to all groups and served similar functions. Frontier settlers used folklore to extol bravery, especially that displayed by one of their own against stronger competitors. They turned to it as a mechanism to poke fun at an attributed effeminacy of other races, who perhaps could not perform as capably on the ranch, in the mines, or on the railroad tracks. Plain folks, as did others in different parts of the country, might also salute their own wisdom and practicality through folktales. Or they might teach children of the tenacity inherent in their cultural system: such resilience explained community endurance through the ages and fortitude and forbearance under duress.

As has been the case universally with populations lacking education, Mexican settlers turned to oral tradition as a substitute for the written word. Throughout the West, people appreciated the preservation of history, of legends, and of religious beliefs via the spoken word. Indeed, even the literate population enjoyed reading orally transmitted poetry or stories published in newspapers and other sources, while members of the working class relished listening to their literate neighbors read them those same printed pieces.[30] When people acquired reading abilities by attending public schools, the old ways of verbal diffusion still persisted, as with folklore.

Mexicans also used folklore to pass on folktales about historical events or buried treasures, to try to explain the supernatural, or to teach the young survival skills as well as the rules of morality and of proper conduct. Folklore also encompassed *corridos;* these folkloric ballads had their origins in the Spanish romances, though structurally and in substance they belonged very much to the experiences of the New World. Set to music and accompanied by a guitar or fiddle, corridos related new experiences in the West. Some recounted the adventures of Mexicans engaged in cattle drives, of brave men who had vanquished great odds, or of Mexicans who stood up to frontier injustice.[31]

Did the identity people wished for themselves persevere undisturbed as cultures skirmished on the frontier? Forces tugged at them not to retreat from their cultural base. For one thing, peers insisted on conformity. Compatriots pressured potential defectors into the fold through ostracism, ridicule, and even intimidation. Those understanding the need for biculturation and wishing to become acquainted with the ways of the Anglo Americans (and fellow community members invariably sought out such persons as intermediaries between their own minority societies and the mainstream structure) risked earning the epithet of cultural turncoat. Purists saw such types as frauds corrupting the language, customs, beliefs, and fashions of the mother culture (*pochos* in Spanish). For cultural nationalists, identifying with something other than a member of the in-group meant forsaking one's own. Some of those making the conversion might no longer be trusted in the barrio, the black quarter, or the transplanted Chinatown. Thus, Westerners seldom intentionally set out on the road of borrowing from neighboring cultures.

Also weighing on those contemplating conversion was the known contempt different people on the frontier had for one another. Especially racist were white Americans, who despite their professed tolerance saw little of a palatable nature in what minority groups offered. The latter's foods, fashions, entertainment, and religious thinking, after all, were aspects identifiable with conquered, inferior, or lower-class working people. Moreover, whites held strong ethnocentric feelings about their own civilization and saw Africans, Chinese, and Mexicans as practitioners of strange ways of life. Even if whites conceded that the three minorities descended from once majestic civilizations, that fact had no bearing on the present. Whites now had surpassed the advances of previous civilizations and their racial superiority was, to them, incontestable in the West.

But the social environment could well take any racist or nationalist in unanticipated directions. This experience happened to whites, blacks, and Mexicans in 1880 as they faced unique circumstances in Presidio County (modern-day Brewster, Jeff Davis, and Presidio counties). Located in far west Texas (between San Antonio and El Paso), the region was an economically struggling area requiring all present to work together for simple existence. Much of life revolved around small-scale ranching there as well as around Fort Davis, a military installation staffed primarily by Buffalo Soldiers and white officers. The county's total population in 1880 stood at close to three thousand, with 73 percent being Mexican (most of it Mexico-born), 16 percent black, and 9 percent white. All had to reach a rapprochement with the others, and though the amount of cultural exchange there cannot be known, much mixing of the races (social, economic, and sexual) did occur. Skewed sex ratios (for whites and blacks) required contact with the predominantly Mexican population, so that half of all married Anglos (approximately forty-five men) had Mexican wives, and 45 percent of married black soldiers (about eleven men) also had Mexican spouses. In addition, there were illicit unions reported by the census takers that year, again involving white and black men cohabiting with Mexican women. At a time when frontier conditions demanded cooperation and no race could really assert authority over the others, small alliances took form in the social, political, and economic arenas.

Thus all three races had to modify their imported identities to exist as part of a tricultural community. Records do not exist to indicate the manner in which each group culturally accommodated the other; did Spanish become the language of communication, or did Mexicans accept aspects of black culture? Indeed, historians are unable to determine what happened to those involved in interracial marriages or liaisons (did the women accompany their husbands when the men left the region?) or even what became of the descendants of these unions. From the fact that partnerships of various types were not extraordinary as of 1880, however, it may be speculated that the social environment in Presidio County did in fact alter the homeland identity of all subjects involved. Whatever shift occurred proved to be only temporary, as the soldiers left by 1885 and an increased number of whites arrived in far west Texas after that time to assert the political and economic authority they had earlier lacked.[32]

A wide range of factors, then, determined the way people referenced themselves on the frontier during the period from 1848 to 1890. On the one hand, there stood appreciation for what they brought from the homeland, but on the other, competition and survival demanded compromises. To what degree people broadened the province of culture to incorporate mutual beliefs, traditions, and institutions is impossible to quantify. Nonetheless, interaction on the political and economic planes, though strained, could not help but reconfigure cultural identity and reshape people into something other than what they had been upon entering the frontier. Such was the case for ones who opted for conversion to another religion, as did a few Chinese Americans in San Francisco whom Christian proselytizers persuaded to join an interdenominational organization established there in 1871. Called the *Zhengdaohui*, the association of Chinese Christians had as its purpose teaching the Christian word in Chinatown to save Chinese souls. The group developed leaders, made its own decisions, and set the direction of the organization until it withered away during the 1920s.[33]

Material accoutrements borrowed from others also recast personal identity. Something as mundane as the adoption of American clothing was bound to have a deep personal impact, as it might have had on the Chinese whose traditional fashions came to be inappropriate on the frontier. The preference in China for common people was overalls, comfortable homespun shirts, and a wide-brimmed dark hat. The tendency in the West among both Chinese men and women was still to use loose clothing—a long blue or gray cotton shirt that clung to the knees and wide comfortable pants—but the type of work to be done in the mining camps or railroad lines demanded adaptation. Thus, Chinese workers quickly discarded bamboo/straw headwear or skullcaps for felt-brimmed hats; their sandals, slippers, or wooden shoes for leather boots that protected their feet from rocks, harsh flora, or snow; and their native attire for flannel shirts and tighter fitting trousers.[34]

The Chinese also moved away—certainly out in the remote frontier regions—from the type of housing they occupied in the homeland. In the mining camps of the Rocky Mountains, the Chinese rented the saltbox homes prevalent in the Boise Basin. An American invention from New England brought West by white settlers, these structures proved to be perfectly suitable for the Chinese. When the Chinese built their own "Chinatown" in Idaho City, they modeled their quarters on the local saltbox houses, which were nothing more than two-room lumber cabins partitioned into a living room and a bedroom.[35]

Adaptive identity was also evident in the U.S. commemorative holidays that people of Mexican descent accepted. Most remained aficionados of Mexican holidays (such as the *Diez y Seis* and the *Cinco de Mayo*) and of Mexican patriots (such as Miguel Hidalgo and Benito Juárez), even while recognizing their allegiance to the United States. At an 1873 Mexican Independence Day commemoration in Santa Barbara, California, an orator declared: "We are Mexicans, almost all of us here present at this reunion or celebration, by our fathers or ancestors, although we are now under a neighboring nation's flag to which we owe respect. Notwithstanding this respect does not prevent us from remembering our Mexican anniversary."[36] And respect for the U.S. colors was expressed in public spirit during various American gala days, such as the U.S. Centennial of 1876, yearly Independence Day observations, or even Washington's birthday in February.[37]

Ultimately, racial identity remained close to its roots. For instance, most Westerners did not defect en masse into the religious columns of the others. For the most part, all groups continued to identify with the spiritual teachings of their forefathers. African Americans, for their part, successfully transplanted most of their churches from the East, among them the African Methodist Episcopal Church. In the late eighteenth century, African American Methodists in the U.S. North had sought to escape the domination of white religious leaders by establishing parallel churches based on Methodist doctrine. A number of black Methodist congregations thus came together in Pennsylvania in the early nineteenth century to form the African Methodist Episcopal (AME) Church, and the church went on to become the most popular Methodist denomination among blacks in the entire United States.[38]

As a predominantly African American religious institution, the AME Church came to be a fixture in many black communities out West, and the African American religious took special interest not solely in ministering to the faithful but in embellishing the church's physical dimensions. Blacks in San Francisco during the 1860s launched special fundraising efforts to build a structure with which they might identify; the result was a magnificent building featuring gothic piers and "bells, a belfry, and organ" that accentuated its stately image.[39] Barney Fletcher, a former slave from Maryland who became a major figure in western evangelism, worked on behalf of the AME.[40]

If the AME church had been their own in the East, it remained part of African American identity in the West, as blacks, just like others on the frontier, held fast to the ways and traditions left back home. Old beliefs that constituted the sense of community were too much ingrained to be voided even in remote places. True enough that the frontier fostered variations from the core culture, as settlers, especially ones of the second generation, embraced elements from outsiders. It was even possible for Westerners to assume dual identities, integrating the patriotism of the new place while avowing allegiance to the old heritage. But the overwhelming number of folks on the trans-Mississippi region, regardless of color, had gone West for the sake of material betterment, not to assume a wholly different identity in the process.

EPILOGUE

The Racial Frontier

In late 1869, at the high tide of Radical Reconstruction in Texas, fourteen African Americans won election to the Texas legislature. Their victory came only four years after "Juneteenth" (June 19, 1865, the day in which federal forces declared slavery at an end in the state), and shortly after African Americans in the state had the opportunity to learn firsthand of American politics and act on their own behalf. In Austin, the fourteen men acquitted themselves fairly well despite their status as former slaves (only two of them had been free blacks). All had apparently pursued a scrupulous regimen for self-advancement, as only three were illiterate, and each had amassed political experience of some kind or another following the ending of the Civil War. The legislators made their living as mechanics, blacksmiths, carpenters, teamsters, farmers, and preachers, but their common acumen for politics had cast them into leadership roles as organizers, voter registrars, educators for the freedmen, and the like. When the Republican Party surfaced in Texas in 1867, they joined its ranks and attended party confabs and conventions; four had even won election to the state constitutional convention of 1868–1869. Once at the State House in Austin, they voted collectively on issues relevant to the African American population of the state, among them programs for educational equality and police protection.[1]

As did the black legislators, the Chinese also quickly adapted to frontier circumstances; within years after their arrival in the West they had become quite knowledgeable about American horticulture and had made Chinese cropping a successful endeavor. White farmers in California had little appreciation for mustard, for instance, seeing the plants as not much more than weeds. But mustard had always been an ingredient in the Chinese diet; moreover, the Chinese knew that mustard seeds contained an oil ideal for seasoning. During the 1860s, according to lore, a Chinese American entrepreneur in the Monterey Bay region of California by the name of "Poison Jack" had acquired the "weeds" from local Anglo farmers (to whom he hired out to poison ground squirrels), had used his crew to extract the seeds from the plants, and had then sold the seeds to a French retail merchant for an immense profit (it happened that at that moment there existed a worldwide mustard seed shortage). Learning from example, Anglo farmers in the area by the 1870s and 1880s had turned to planting mustard for its seed and had made the investment a growing concern.[2] But harvesting mustard was not the only example of Chinese entrepreneurship reconciled with the American frontier environment. The Asians also discovered new, highly profitable crops to cultivate. In northern California, for instance, Chinese farmers renounced the sweet potato (a traditional crop in China) and opted for the Irish potato, which rendered them a higher profit margin.[3]

In contrast to quick (and eager) adaptation to the political and economic systems, people of color balked at becoming "cultural Americans." Preferring attachment to the ways of the homeland, they abided by old customs, though conceding change in the social environment. Tradition defining gender roles, for one, endured. The definition articulated by the editor of an Arizona newspaper, as an example, reflected the views most Western males held, regardless of their race. Ignacio Bonillas's comments, published in *El Fronterizo* in the summer of 1882, spoke more specifically for Mexican men. For him, custom called for women to be noble: "The mother is the priestess, the mother has a great mission to fulfill on earth, to form souls through her virtue." Custom entrusted women with specific responsibilities toward the family: to provide for the spiritual education, well-being, and happiness of the children and to offer moral support to the husband during times of travail. For Bonillas, the wife was "a balm for [her husband's] cares, a counsel for all his worries, surrounding him with her tender sisterly soul."

But not all endorsed this custom, especially given the frontier's equalizing force. Such was the case with a woman contributor to *El Fronterizo* in 1883. Certainly male subordination could not be justified by the Bible, she noted. If anything, man was the weaker creature. "Adam was the first coward because when God asked him, 'Have you eaten of the forbidden fruit?' Adam answered while hiding behind Eve." Given that show of cowardice, men hardly deserved a right to proclaim domination. She added: "Men are like lit cigars, they show more smoke than fire." As to custom: "If you have committed enough foolishness and have become conceited enough and have mocked and cursed women sufficiently then hold your nose animal!"[4]

Identity for the mass of those on the frontier remained largely "ethnic," as people accepted the salience of their native/traditional upbringing. Culture trumped race, as is evident in the story of Ignacia Cano and her children. In 1849, Ignacia (daughter of a Mexico-born mine owner in New Mexico) married Benjamin Franklin Read, an American who arrived with the army of occupation that conquered the New Mexico territory in 1846. Read died a decade later, leaving Ignacia with three boys to raise on her own. All the youths grew up in a Mexican ambiance, raised by their mother and close relatives who always made themselves available to provide the widow with a helping hand. Ignacia struggled to put the boys through school, but all finished their education and became respected attorneys. At least two of them married Mexican women, and Ignacia herself remarried, this time to an Hispano named Mateo Ortiz.

One of her sons was famed New Mexico historian Benjamín (Maurice) Read, whose Anglo name belied his identity as a Mexicano. Born in 1853, Benjamín Read married three times; all his marriages were to Mexican women who unfortunately died, leaving him to raise his own children alone as had his mother, Ignacia. He was a Catholic and a native Spanish-speaker who preferred communicating (he was an eloquent orator) and writing in his mother tongue (although he was fluent in English as well). During a professional career that spanned several decades (into the twentieth century), Benjamín Read the lawyer served New Mexico in numerous capacities, among them translator, legislator, and advocate for Nuevo Mexicano history. His numerous works, most of them written in Spanish, relied on the original documents of the pre-1848 period and made a subtle plea for recognition of the nuevo mexicanos' ethnic identity.[5] Read's father was white, but his mother's culture prevailed.

We return to the question posed in the introduction to this book: "What generally resulted when different racial groups converged on the Western frontier?" As the above stories illustrate, the outcome was adjustment if necessity dictated, and reluctant modification otherwise. Like the black legislators, people were fully capable of comprehending (in rather quick time) and participating in a political system they admired, one they believed encompassing enough to see to their protection. Many held similar views of the economic system and preferred it to the one left behind. By applying innate ingenuity to the land, or to any industry for that matter, they could hasten earning a living wage.

Adopting new customs and turning their back on their national character was another matter, however. Some customs appeared old-fashioned, restrictive, and inapplicable to the West, but as a corps of beliefs they outlasted the nineteenth-century frontier era. The same was true of identity: Western people of color accepted tenets of other cultures, but their loyalty generally remained with the way of life that nourished them in segregated areas and defined them as a racial unit. This maintenance of cultural baggage and identity among minority groups did not deviate substantially from the practice of Anglo Americans, who similarly attempted to sink old roots in new environments. To put things in perspective, minority peoples collectively never numbered more than 10 percent of the greater population beyond the Mississippi. Yet their imprint on the West far exceeded that figure, for unquestionably the frontier took the shape of many colors.

NOTES

Introduction

1. Harold E. Driver, *Indians of North America* (Chicago: University of Chicago Press, 1961), p. 602.

2. Other historians have already attempted a look at these actors, among them Sucheng Chan et al. in *Peoples of Color in the American West* (Lexington, Mass.: D. C. Heath and Co., 1994).

3. David J. Weber and Jane M. Rausch (eds.), *Where Cultures Meet: Frontiers in Latin American History* (Wilmington, Del.: SR Books, 1994), p. xiv. Also see Frederick C. Luebke, "Ethnic Minority Groups in the American West," in *Historians and the American West*, ed. Michael P. Malone (Lincoln: University of Nebraska Press, 1983), p. 393.

4. See chapter 1, table 2.

5. *Texas State Gazette*, Austin, Texas, September 9, 1854, p. 4; Arnoldo De León, *They Called Them Greasers: Anglo Attitudes toward Mexicans in Texas, 1821–1900* (Austin: University of Texas Press, 1983), pp. 49–53.

6. Among studies that inform this argument would be Weber and Rausch (eds.), *Where Cultures Meet;* Ray Allen Billington, *America's Frontier Heritage* (Albuquerque: University of New Mexico Press, 1974); Richard W. Etulain, *Writing Western History: Essays on Major Western Historians* (Albuquerque: University of New Mexico Press, 1991); Gerald D. Nash, *Creating the West: Historical Interpretations, 1890–1990* (Albuquerque: University of New Mexico Press, 1991); Wilbur R. Jacobs, *On Turner's Trail: One Hundred Years of Writing Western History* (Lawrence: University Press of Kansas, 1994); Patricia Limerick et al., (eds.), *Trails: Towards a New Western History* (Lawrence: University Press of Kansas, 1991); Patricia Limerick, *The Legacy of Conquest: The Unbroken Past of the American West* (New York: Norton, 1988).

7. Billington, *America's Frontier Heritage,* pp. 37–38.

8. Robert G. Athearn, *In Search of Canaan: Black Migration to Kansas, 1879–1880* (Lawrence: The Regents Press of Kansas, 1978), p. 81.

9. Ibid., pp. 81–82.

10. Thomas Cooper Cox, *Blacks in Topeka, Kansas, 1865–1915: Social History* (Baton Rouge: Louisiana State University Press, 1982), pp. 37–45 and chapter 3; Billy D. Higgins, "Negro Thought and the Exodus of 1879," *Phylon* 32 (1971): 42;

Nudie E. Williams, "Black Newspapers and the Exodusters of 1879," *Kansas History* (winter 1985–1986): 219–20, 222; William L. Katz, *The Black West* (New York: Doubleday, 1973), pp. 170–75.

Chapter 1

1. June Mei, "Socio-Economic Origins of Emigration, Guangdong to California, 1850–1882," *Modern China* 5 (October 1979): 484, 493–98; Michael H. Hunt, *The Making of a Special Relationship: The United States and China to 1914* (New York: Columbia University Press, 1983), p. 64; Kil Young Zo, *Chinese Emigration into the United States, 1850–1880* (New York: Arno Press, 1978), pp. 88–89, 91–92, 114, 116; H. Brett Melendy, *The Oriental Americans* (New York: Twayne Publishers, Inc., 1972), pp. 11, 15; Jack Chen, *The Chinese of America: From the Beginnings to the Present* (San Francisco: Harper and Row, 1980), p. 62.

Some authors say "Gold Mountain" is a reference to California or to San Francisco. See for example Zo, *Chinese Emigration into the United States*, pp. 88, 92; and Sucheng Chan, *Asian Americans: An Interpretive History* (Boston: Twayne Publishers, 1991), p. 28. But others say it refers to the United States as a whole. See as examples Diane Mei Lin Mark and Ginger Chih, *A Place Called Chinese America* (Dubuque, Iowa: Kendall/Hunt Publishing Co., 1982), p. 6; Quintard Taylor, *The Forging of a Black Community: Seattle's Central District from 1870 through the Civil Rights Era* (Seattle: University of Washington Press, 1994), p. 111.

2. Thomas W. Chinn, H. Mark Lai, and Philip P. Choy, *A History of the Chinese in California: A Syllabus* (San Francisco: Chinese Historical Society of America, 1969), pp. 2, 4; Sucheng Chan, *This Bittersweet Soil: The Chinese in California Agriculture, 1860–1910* (Berkeley: University of California Press, 1986), pp. 16–18; Chen, *The Chinese of America*, pp. 16, 18; Mei, "Socio-economic Origins of Emigration," pp. 463–66; Zo, *Chinese Emigration into the United States*, pp. 55–56; Melendy, *The Oriental Americans*, pp. 2, 11–12; Hunt, *The Making of a Special Relationship*, pp. 61–64, 72; Robert R. Swartout, Jr., "Kwangtung to Big Sky: The Chinese in Montana, 1864–1900," *Montana, The Magazine of Western History* 38 (winter 1988): 44; Joseph W. Stephens, "A Quantitative History of Chinatown, San Francisco, 1870 and 1880," in *The Life, Influence, and Role of the Chinese in the United States, 1776–1960*, ed. Chinese Historical Society of America (San Francisco: Chinese Historical Society of America, 1976), pp. 82–85.

3. Sucheng Chan, *Asian Californians* (San Francisco: MTL/Boyd and Fraser, 1991), pp. 10–12; Mei, "Socio-economic Origins of Emigration," pp. 469–71; Chen, *The Chinese of America*, pp. 7–9, 16; Tricia Knoll, *Becoming Americans: Asian*

Sojourners, Immigrants, and Refugees in the Western United States (Portland: Coast-to-Coast Books, 1982), pp. 12–13; Chinn, Lai, and Choy, *A History of the Chinese in California*, pp. 11–12.

4. Chan, *Bittersweet Soil*, pp. 19–20, 22–23; Chan, *Asian Californians*, pp. 12–13; Mei, "Socio-economic Origins of Emigration," pp. 468, 470, 471, 492–93, 496; Zo, *Chinese Emigration into the United States*, pp. 62, 64, 78; Chen, *The Chinese of America*, p. 8; Hunt, *The Making of a Special Relationship*, p. 63; Shih-Shan Henry Tsai, *The Chinese Experience in America* (Bloomington: Indiana University Press, 1986), pp. 2–3.

5. Chan, *Bittersweet Soil*, pp. 19–20; Chan, *Asian Californians*, pp. 12–13; Liping Zhu, *A Chinaman's Chance: The Chinese in the Rocky Mountain Mining Frontier* (Niwot, Colo.: University of Colorado Press, 1997), pp. 20–21; Hunt, *The Making of A Special Relationship*, p. 63; Chinn, Lai, and Choy, *A History of the Chinese in California*, pp. 11, 12 (note 2), 22; Zo, *Chinese Emigration into the United States*, pp. 114, 119, 120–21, 154–60, 198; Mei, "Socio-economic Origins of Emigration," pp. 472–73; Mark and Chih, *A Place Called Chinese America*, p. 4.

6. Yong Chen, "The Internal Origins of Chinese Emigration to California Reconsidered," *Western Historical Quarterly* 28 (winter 1997): 521–46.

7. Billington, *America's Frontier Heritage*, pp. 31–33.

8. Mei, "Socio-economic Origins of Emigration," pp. 484, 494–98; Zo, *Chinese Emigration into the United States*, pp. 88–89, 91–92, 114, 116, 165; Hunt, *The Making of a Special Relationship*, p. 64; Melendy, *The Oriental Americans*, p. 15; Stanford M. Lyman, *The Asian in the West* (Reno: Desert Research Institute, University of Nevada, 1970), p. 11; Chen, *The Chinese of America*, p. 62; Bill Ong Hing, *Making and Remaking Asian America through Immigration Policy, 1850–1990* (Stanford, Calif.: Stanford University Press, 1993), pp. 20–21.

9. Gunther Barth, *Bitter Strength: A History of Chinese in the United States, 1850–1870* (Cambridge: Harvard University Press, 1964), pp. 55–57; Hunt, *The Making of a Special Relationship*, p. 65; Zo, *Chinese Emigration into the United States*, pp. 65–66, 93–94, 95–96, 199; Melendy, *The Oriental Americans*, pp. 14, 19; Lyman, *Asians in the West*, p. 12; Chinn, Lai, and Choy, *A History of the Chinese in California*, p. 15; Mark and Chih, *A Place Called Chinese America*, p. 5; Chen, *The Chinese of America*, p. 26; Zhu, *Chinaman's Chance*, pp. 20–21.

10. Barth, *Bitter Strength*, p. 69; Melendy, *The Oriental Americans*, p. 21; Chinn, Lai, and Choy, *A History of the Chinese in California*, p. 16; Mei, Mark, and Chih, *A Place Called Chinese America*, p. 7; Chen, *The Chinese of America*, pp. 6, 26; Zo, *Chinese Emigration into the United States*, pp. 106, 109, 115.

11.   Chan, *Bittersweet Soil,* pp. 26–27; Barth, *Bitter Strength,* pp. 65–76; Zo, *Chinese Emigration into the United States,* pp. 91, 106, 107; Chinn, Lai, and Choy, *A History of the Chinese in California,* p. 16; Melendy, *The Oriental Americans,* p. 22; Chen, *The Chinese of America,* p. 23; Mark and Chih, *A Place Called Chinese America,* p. 7.

12.   Chinn, Lai, and Choy, *A History of the Chinese in California,* p. 16; Lyman, *Asians in the West,* p. 12; Knoll, *Becoming Americans,* p. 22; Melendy, *The Oriental Americans,* pp. 19, 71, 73–74; Chan, *Bittersweet Soil,* p. 32; Thomas W. Chinn, *Bridging the Pacific: San Francisco Chinatown and Its People* (San Francisco: Chinese Historical Society of America, 1989), pp. 4–5; Hunt, *The Making of a Special Relationship,* pp. 65–66; Chen, *The Chinese of America,* p. 27.

13.   Judy Yung, *Unbound Feet: A Social History of Chinese Women in San Francisco* (Berkeley: University of California Press, 1995), p. 48; Barth, *Bitter Strength,* pp. 63–64; Chinn, Lai, and Choy, *A History of the Chinese in California,* pp. 8, 9; Melendy, *The Oriental Americans,* p. 15; Chen, *The Chinese of America,* p. 11; S. W. King, *Chinese of American Life: Some Aspects of Their History, Status, Problems and Contributions* (Seattle: University of Washington Press, 1962), p. 65.

14.   Chan, *Bittersweet Soil,* pp. 42–44, 45, 47–51, 160; Mark and Chih, *A Place Called Chinese America,* pp. 7, 8; Lyman, *Asians in the West,* p. 15; Chinn, Lai, and Choy, *A History of the Chinese in California,* p. 23; *Report on Population of the United States at the Eleventh Census: 1890, Part I,* "General Tables," table 16: "Chinese Population by Counties: 1870–1890" (Washington, D.C.: Government Printing Office, 1895), pp. 440–41.

15.   Barth, *Bitter Strength,* pp. 185–86; Chan, *Bittersweet Soil,* pp. 44–45; Lyman, *Asians in the West,* p. 14; Mark and Chih, *A Place Called Chinese America,* pp. 20, 22; Doug and Art Chin, *Up Hill: The Settlement and Diffusion of the Chinese in Seattle, Washington* (Seattle: Shorey Original Publications, 1973), pp. 3, 8–9, 16; Taylor, *Forging of a Black Community,* pp. 110–11; Swartout, "Kwangtung to Big Sky," pp. 44–45; John R. Wunder, "Land and Chinese in Frontier Montana," *Montana, The Magazine of Western History* 30 (1980): 20, 22; Liping Zhu, "How the Other Half Lived: Chinese Daily Life in Boise Basin Mining Camps," *Idaho Yesterdays* 38 (winter 1995): 20; Ronald L. James, "Why No Chinamen Are Found in Twin Falls," *Idaho Yesterdays* 36 (winter 1993): 16, 19–23; Russell M. Magnaghi, "Virginia City's Chinese Community, 1860–1880," *Nevada Historical Society Quarterly* 24 (1981): 130–31, 156–57; Loren B. Chan, "The Chinese in Nevada: An Historical Survey, 1856–1870," *Nevada Historical Society Quarterly* 25 (winter 1982): 266–68; Gregg Lee Carter, "Social Demography of the Chinese in Nevada: 1870–1880," *Nevada*

Historical Society Quarterly 28 (summer 1975): 73–74; Grant K. Anderson, "Deadwood's Chinatown," *South Dakota History* 5 (summer 1975): 266–67; Daniel Liestman, "Utah's Chinatowns: The Development and Decline of Extinct Ethnic Enclaves," *Utah Historical Quarterly* 64 (winter 1996): 72–73.

16. Shan, *Bittersweet Soil*, p. 46.

17. *The New Handbook of Texas*, 6 vols. (Austin: Texas State Historical Association, 1996), 3:628.

18. Arthur Corwin, *Immigrants—and Immigrants* (Westport, Conn.: Greenwood Press, 1978), pp. 27–29, 35, 43, 46; Thomas E. Sheridan, *Los Tucsonenses: The Mexican Community in Tucson, 1854–1941* (Tucson: University of Arizona Press, 1986), pp. 77–78; Juan Gómez-Quiñones, *Mexican American Labor, 1790–1990* (Albuquerque: University of New Mexico Press, 1994), p. 26.

19. Oscar J. Martínez, "On the Size of the Chicano Population: New Estimates, 1850–1900," *Aztlán: International Journal of Chicano Studies Research* 6 (spring 1975): 55; Corwin, *Immigrants—and Immigrants*, pp. 25, 27, 28, 43; Sheridan, *Los Tucsonenses*, pp. 76, 167, 268.

20. Martínez, "On the Size of the Chicano Population," pp. 55, 58; Arthur L. Campa, *Hispanic Culture in the Southwest* (Norman: University of Oklahoma Press, 1979), pp. 148–49.

21. Dolores Hayden, "Biddy Mason's Los Angeles, 1856–1891," *California History* 68 (fall 1984): 88–89.

22. W. Sherman Savage, *Blacks in the West* (Westport, Conn.: Greenwood Press, 1976), p. 19; Quintard Taylor, *In Search of the Racial Frontier: African Americans in the American West, 1528–1990* (New York: W. W. Norton, 1998), pp. 202–3; *Report on Population of the United States at the Eleventh Census: 1890*, table 13: "White and Negro Population, by States and Territories, 1850–1890," p. 400. The census puts the number of African Americans in Oklahoma at 2,973, but Savage notes that because of Oklahoma's standing as an Indian territory, records were not accurately kept. His own figure for African Americans in the Sooner State is 21,000 for 1890 (*Blacks in the West*, p. 4).

23. Ruby El Hult, "The Saga of George W. Bush," *Negro Digest* 11 (September 1962). See further Thomas C. Hogg, "Negroes and Their Institutions in Oregon," in *The Northwest Mosaic: Minority Conflicts in the Pacific Northwest*, ed. James A. Halseth and Bruce A. Glasrud (Boulder, Colo.: Pruett Publishing Co., 1977), pp. 69–70; Savage, *Blacks in the West*, p. 11; Katz, *The Black West*, pp. 73–77.

24. Savage, *Blacks in the West*, appendix; *Report on Population . . .* table 13, p. 400.

25. Daniels, *Pioneer Urbanites*, pp. 17, 25, 32; Lawrence B. de Graaf, "Race, Sex, and Region: Black Women in the American West, 1850–1920," *Pacific Historical Review* 49 (May 1980): 286, 290–91.

26. Corwin, *Immigrants—and Immigrants*, pp. 37 note 21, 34; Martínez, "On the Size of the Chicano Population," p. 56.

27. Martínez, "On the Size of the Chicano Population," pp. 55 and 56, table.

28. Melendy, *The Oriental Americans*, p. 12; Chinn, Lai, and Choy, *A History of the Chinese in California*, p. 12.

29. Chinn, Lai, and Choy, *A History of the Chinese in California*, pp. 13, 22; Zo, *Chinese Emigration into the United States*, p. 114; Melendy, *The Oriental Americans*, p. 15; Chen, *The Chinese of America*, p. 268. I arrived at the figure of 91.0 percent by taking the 97,955 Chinese I have listed in table 2 (titled "Racial Populations in the Trans-Mississippi West") and dividing that number by 107,488.

30. Miguel León-Portilla, "The Norteño Variety of Mexican Culture: An Ethno-Historical Approach," in *Plural Society in the Southwest*, ed. Edward M. Spicer and Raymond H. Thompson (Albuquerque: University of New Mexico Press, 1972), pp. 109–14.

31. Barry A. Crouch, "The 'Chords of Love': Legalizing Black Marital and Family Rights in Post-War Texas," *The Journal of Negro History* 79 (fall 1994): 342–43.

Chapter 2

1. Jerry D. Thompson, ed., *Juan Cortina and the Texas-Mexico Frontier, 1859–1877* (El Paso: Texas Western Press, 1994), pp. 1–7; Silvio Zavala, "The Frontiers of Hispanic America," in *The Frontier in Perspective*, ed. Walker D. Wyman and Clifton B. Kroeber (Madison: University of Wisconsin Press, 1965), pp. 49, 50; and León-Portilla, "The Norteño Variety of Mexican Culture," pp. 112–13.

2. David J. Weber, *The Mexican Frontier, 1821–1848: The American Southwest under Mexico* (Albuquerque: University of New Mexico Press, 1982), pp. 32, 35–36, 40, 41, 280.

3. Thompson, *Juan Cortina and the Texas-Mexico Border*, pp. 1, 11–12.

4. Ibid., pp. 12, 23–28.

5. Leigh Dana Johnsen, "Equal Rights and the 'Heathen Chinee': Black Activism in San Francisco," *Western Historical Quarterly* 11 (January 1980).

6. Raymund Paredes, "The Origins of Anti-Mexican Sentiment in the United States," in *New Directions in Chicano Scholarship*, ed. Ricardo Romo and

Raymund Paredes (La Jolla: University of California at San Diego, 1978), pp. 139–66; Arnoldo De León, *The Mexican Image in Nineteenth Century Texas* (Boston: American Press, 1982), pp. 8–14.

7. George G. Smith, *The Life and Times of George Foster Pierce* (Sparta, Ga.: Hancock Publishing Co., 1888), pp. 375–76.

8. Albert Camarillo, *Chicanos in a Changing Society: From Mexican Pueblos to American Barrios in Santa Barbara and Southern California* (Cambridge: Harvard University Press, 1979), p. 15; Richard Nostrand, *The Hispano Homeland* (Norman: University of Oklahoma Press, 1992), p. 106; De León, *They Called Them Greasers,* chapters 3 and 4; Douglas Monroy, *Thrown Among Strangers: The Making of Mexican Culture in Frontier California* (Berkeley: University of California Press, 1990), p. 206; Sheridan, *Los Tucsonenses,* p. 32; and Leonard Pitt, *The Decline of the Californios: A Social History of the Spanish-Speaking Californians, 1846–1900* (Berkeley: University of California Press, 1966), p. 71.

9. *New Handbook of Texas,* 4:873–74. Hobart Huson, *Refugio: A Comprehensive History of Refugio County from Aboriginal Times to 1955,* 2 vols. (Woodsboro, Tex.: The Rooke Foundation, Inc., 1956), 2:206–12; San Antonio *Express,* June 12, 1874, p. 2; June 13, 1874, p. 2; June 16, 1874, p. 2.

10. John R. Wunder, "Anti-Chinese Violence in the American West, 1850–1910," in *Law for the Elephant, Law for the Beaver: Essays in the Legal History of the North American West,* ed. John McLaren, Hamar Foster, and Chet Orloff (Pasadena, Calif.: Ninth Judicial Circuit Historical Society, 1992), pp. 225–28; Ron T. Wortman, "Denver's Anti-Chinese Riot, 1880," *The Colorado Magazine* 42 (fall 1965): 275–91 (quote is from p. 285).

11. Hunt, *The Making of a Special Relationship,* pp. 81–82; Tsai, *The Chinese Experience in America,* pp. 70–72; Taylor, *Forging of a Black Community,* pp. 111–12; Clayton D. Laurie, "'The Chinese Must Go': The United States Army and the Anti-Chinese Riots in Washington Territory," *Pacific Northwest Quarterly* 81 (January 1990): 24–25, 27–28; Wunder, "Anti-Chinese Violence," 216–17, 222; Margaret K. Holden, "Gender and Protest Ideology: Sue Ross Keenan and the Oregon Anti-Chinese Movement," *Western Legal History: The Journal of the Ninth Judicial District* (summer/fall, 1994): 240–42.

12. Elizabeth McLagan, *A Peculiar Paradise: A History of Blacks in Oregon, 1788–1940* (Portland, Oreg.: The Georgian Press, 1980), pp. 26, 28; Savage, *Blacks in the West,* pp. 139, 141; Rudolph M. Lapp, *Blacks in Gold Rush California* (New Haven: Yale University Press, 1977), pp. 239–40; Kenneth G. Goode, *California's Black Pioneers: A Brief Historical Survey* (Santa Barbara, Calif.: McNelly and

Loftin Publishers, 1974), pp. 45, 48–49; Michael S. Coray, "Negro and Mulatto in the Pacific West, 1850–1860: Changing Patterns of Black Population Growth," *The Pacific Historian* 29 (winter 1985): 19–20; Thomas C. Hogg, "Negroes and Their Institutions in Oregon," in *The Northwest Mosaic: Minority Conflicts in Pacific Northwest History,* ed. James A. Halseth and Bruce A. Glasrud (Boulder, Colo.: Pruett Publishing Co., 1977), pp. 70, 71; K. Keith Richard, "Unwelcomed Settlers: Blacks and Mulatto Oregon Pioneers, Part II," *Oregon Historical Quarterly* 84 (summer 1983): 32, 36; Taylor, *In Search of the Racial Frontier,* pp. 76–77.

13. Savage, *Blacks in the West,* pp. 25, 34, 35, 38, 43; J. Max Bond, *The Negro in Los Angeles* (San Francisco: R & E Research Associates, 1972), p. 7; Tomás Almaguer, *Racial Fault Lines: The Historical Origins of White Supremacy in California* (Berkeley: University of California, 1994), p. 39; Katz, *The Black West,* p. 134. Iowa even had an underground railroad to assist slaves in escaping into Canada. Glenda Riley, *Frontierswomen: The Iowa Experience* (Ames: Iowa State University Press, 1981), p. 94.

14. Newell G. Bringhurst, "The 'Descendants of Ham' in Zion: Discrimination Against Blacks Along the Shifting Mormon Frontier, 1830–1920," *Nevada Historical Society Quarterly* 24 (winter 1981): 309–11; Newell G. Bringhurst, *Saints, Slaves, and Blacks: The Changing Place of Black People Within Mormonism* (Westport, Conn.: Greenwood Press, 1981), pp. 68–69, 73; Ronald Gerald Coleman, "A History of Blacks in Utah, 1825–1910" (Ph.D. diss., University of Utah, 1980), pp. 49–51, 60–61; Taylor, *In Search of the Racial Frontier,* pp. 53–54, 62, 71; Riley, *Frontierswomen,* pp. 91, 93; Hogg, "Negroes and Their Institutions in Oregon," p. 71; Savage, *Blacks in the West,* pp. 26, 139; Randall B. Woods, "Integration, Exclusion, or Segregation? The 'Color Line' in Kansas, 1878–1900," *Western Historical Quarterly* 14 (April 1983): 192; Savage, *Blacks in the West,* p. 139; Goode, *California's Black Pioneers,* pp. 79, 80; Almaguer, *Racial Fault Lines,* p. 38; Daniels, *Pioneer Urbanites,* p. 107; McLagan, *A Peculiar Paradise,* p. 52; William Hanchett, "Yankee Law and the Negro in Nevada, 1861–1869," *The Western Humanities* 10 (1956): 242; Elmer R. Rusco, "*Good Time Coming? Black Nevadans in the Nineteenth Century* (Westport, Conn.: Greenwood Press, 1975), p. 21.

15. Coray, "Negro and Mulatto in the Pacific West," p. 19; Thomas Clark Hogg, "Negroes and Their Institutions in Oregon," *Phylon* 30 (fall 1969): 71; Savage, *Blacks in the West,* pp. 139, 188; Daniels, *Pioneer Urbanites,* p. 107; Hanchett, "Yankee Law and the Negro in Nevada," p. 243; Coleman, "A History of Blacks in Utah," p. 50; Lapp, *Blacks in Gold Rush California,* pp. 268–69.

16. Goode, *California's Black Pioneers,* pp. 86–88. Compare with the discussion

in Lynn M. Hudson, "When 'Mammy' Becomes a Millionaire: Mary Ellen Pleasant, An African American Entrepreneur" (Ph.D. diss., Indiana University, 1996), pp. 83–94.

17. Savage, *Blacks in the West,* pp. 139, 146, 147, 148–49; Bond, *The Negro in Los Angeles,* p. 8; Almaguer, *Racial Faultlines,* p. 38.

18. Goode, *California's Black Pioneers,* pp. 75–78; Delilah Beasley, *The Negro Trailblazers of California* (Los Angeles: Times Mirror Printing and Binding House, 1919), pp. 54–60; Lapp, *Blacks in Gold Rush California,* chapter 8.

19. Savage, *Blacks in the West,* p. 139; McLagan, *A Peculiar Paradise,* pp. 61, 64; Rusco, *"Good Time Coming?"* pp. 22–28, 34, 52–53; Michael Coray, "African Americans in Nevada," *Nevada Historical Society Quarterly* 35 (winter 1992): 242; Riley, *Frontierswomen,* p. 93.

20. Coleman, "A History of Blacks in Utah," pp. 55, 61; Bringhurst, "'Descendants of Ham' in Zion," p. 38; Bond, *The Negro in Los Angeles,* p. 8; Hogg, "Negroes and Their Institutions in Oregon," p. 71; Rusco, *"Good Time Coming?"* pp. 23, 24, 46–48, 58; Cox, *Blacks in Topeka, Kansas,* pp. 26–27; Taylor, *In Search of the Racial Frontier,* p. 126; Sara L. Bernson and Robert J. Eggers, "Black People in South Dakota History," *South Dakota History* 7 (summer 1977): 243.

21. Savage, *Blacks in the West,* pp. 189, 190; McLagan, *A Peculiar Paradise,* pp. 64, 69; Richard, "Unwelcomed Settlers," pp. 44, 55; Rusco, *"Good Time Coming?"* pp. 23, 70; Bringhurst, "'Descendants of Ham' in Zion," p. 312.

22. Goode, *California's Black Pioneers,* pp. 83–85; Coray, "African Americans in Nevada," p. 241; Savage, *Blacks in the West,* pp. 152–54; McLagan, *A Peculiar Paradise,* pp. 64, 72; Cox, *Blacks in Topeka, Kansas,* pp. 27–29, 33–34, 113; J. W. Smurr, "Jim Crow Out West," in *Historical Essays on Montana and the Northwest,* ed. J. W. Smurr and K. Ross Toole (Helena, Mont.: The Western Press, Historical Society of Montana, 1957), pp. 149, 150, 153, 167, 169, 172; Hanchett, "Yankee Law and the Negro in Nevada," p. 246; Riley, *Frontierswomen,* p. 93; Woods, "Integration, Exclusion, or Segregation?" pp. 186–88; Taylor, *In Search of the Racial Frontier,* p. 216.

23. Rusco, *"Good Time Coming?"* pp. 204–6; Cox, *Blacks in Topeka, Kansas,* pp. 117–19; Randall B. Woods, *A Black Odyssey: John Lewis Waller and the Promise of American Life, 1878–1900* (Lawrence: Regents Press of Kansas, 1981), pp. 66–70.

24. Wortman, "Denver's Anti-Chinese Riot," p. 291.

25. Ralph James Mooney, "Matthew Deady and the Federal Judicial Response to Racism in the Early West," *Oregon Law Review* 63 (December 1984).

26. Savage, *Blacks in the West,* pp. 147–50; Katz, *The Black West,* pp. 135–38;

Taylor, *In Search of the Racial Frontier,* pp. 90–92; Lapp, *Blacks in Gold Rush California,* chapters 8–9.

27. Katz, *The Black West,* pp. 139–42. In 1858, Gibbs left California, again to seek his fortune in the gold mines, this time in Canada.

28. Taylor, *In Search of the Racial Frontier,* p. 92; Goode, *California's Black Pioneers,* pp. 74–75, 77, 78.

29. Rusco, *"Good Time Coming?"* p. 70; Eugene C. Berwanger, "Reconstruction on the Frontier: The Equal Rights Struggle in Colorado, 1865–1867," *Pacific Historical Review* 44 (August 1975): 329.

30. Eugene C. Berwanger, "Hardin and Langston: Western Black Spokesmen of the Reconstruction Era," *Journal of Negro History* 64 (spring 1979): 101, 105–12; Savage, *Blacks in the West,* pp. 158, 161–62, 165–66. For a listing of African Americans who won election to territorial or state legislatures throughout the West, see Taylor, *In Search of the Racial Frontier,* pp. 213, 130–33. Katz, *The Black West,* pp. 255–61, gives extensive coverage to McCabe. See further Woods, *A Black Odyssey.*

31. Savage, *Blacks in the West,* pp. 159–60; Berwanger, "Reconstruction on the Frontier"; Eugene C. Berwanger, "William J. Hardin: Colorado Spokesman for Racial Justice, 1863–1873," *The Colorado Magazine* 52 (winter 1975).

32. Roger D. Hardaway, "William Jefferson Hardin: Wyoming's Nineteenth Century Black Legislator," *Annals of Wyoming* 63 (winter 1991): 3, 4, 7, 12.

33. Berlin B. Chandler, "Friends in Time of Need: Republicans and Black Civil Rights in California During the Civil War Era," *Arizona and the West* 24 (winter 1982): 339–40.

34. Charles G. McClain, *In Search of Equality: The Chinese Struggle Against Discrimination in Nineteenth Century America* (Berkeley: University of California Press, 1994), pp. 2–4, 279; Charles G. McClain and Laurene Wu McClain, "The Chinese Contribution to American Law," in Sucheng Chan, *Entry Denied: Exclusion and the Chinese Community in America, 1882–1943* (Philadelphia: Temple University Press, 1991), pp. 3–5, 21; Zhu, *Chinaman's Chance,* pp. 140, 154.

35. McClain, *In Search of Equality,* pp. 133–43.

36. Zhu, *Chinaman's Chance,* pp. 133, 140, 142, 154–55; Victor Low, *The Unimpressible Race: A Century of Educational Struggle by the Chinese in San Francisco* (San Francisco: East/West Publishing Co., 1982), p. 39; Chen, *The Chinese of America,* pp. 142, 139; Tsai, *The Chinese Experience in America,* p. 57; McClain, *In Search of Equality,* pp. 59–63, 76, 163–65; Sucheng Chan, "Exclusion of Chinese Women, 1870–1943," in Chan, *Entry Denied,* pp. 99–105.

37. Tsai, *The Chinese Experience in America,* p. 7; Chen, *The Chinese of*

America, p. 128; McClain, *In Search of Equality,* pp. 30–31; Christian G. Fritz, "A Nineteenth Century 'Habeas Corpus Mill': The Chinese before the Federal Courts in California," *American Journal of Legal History* 32 (October 1988): 351–52.

38. Yanwen Xia, "The Sojourner Myth and Chinese Immigrants in the United States" (Ph.D. diss., Bowling Green State University, 1993), pp. 78, 80, 81; Tsai, *The Chinese Experience in America,* pp. 56–65; Fritz, "Nineteenth Century 'Habeas Corpus Mill,'" p. 353. Not until 1898 did the U.S. Supreme Court *(United States v. Wong Kim Ark)* rule that in accordance with the Fourteenth Amendment any Chinese born in the United States was a citizen. Lucy E. Salyer, *Laws Harsh As Tigers: Chinese Immigrants and the Shaping of Modern Immigration Law* (Chapel Hill: University of North Carolina Press, 1995), p. 99; Brook Thomas, "Chinamen, *U.S. v. Wong Kim Ark* and the Question of Citizenship," *American Quarterly* 50 (September 1998): 689–717.

39. McClain, *In Search of Equality,* pp. 192–98; Xia, "The Sojourner Myth and Chinese Immigrants," pp. 81–82.

40. McClain, *In Search of Equality,* pp. 192–98; Xia, "The Sojourner Myth and the Chinese Immigrants," pp. 83–85; Tsai, *The Chinese Experience in America,* pp. 73–74. The several ways by which the Chinese worked the legal system to circumvent the Chinese Exclusion Act are discussed in Salyer, *Laws Harsh as Tigers,* chapters 1–3.

41. Robert J. Rosenbaum, *Mexicano Resistance in the Southwest: "The Sacred Right of Self-Preservation"* (Austin: University of Texas Press, 1982), chapters 7, 8, 9, and pp. 165, 166; Anselmo Arellano, "The People's Movement: Las Gorras Blancas," in *The Contested Homeland: A Chicano History of New Mexico,* ed. Erlinda Gonzales-Berry and David R. Maciel (Albuquerque: University of New Mexico Press, 2000).

42. Liestman, "Utah's Chinatowns," p. 84.

43. Zhu, *Chinaman's Chance,* pp. 146–50.

Chapter 3

1. See further, Susan Lee Johnson, *Roaring Camp: The Social World of the California Gold Rush* (New York: W. W. Norton and Company, 2000), pp. 243–46.

2. Sheridan, *Los Tucsonenses,* pp. 84–85.

3. Yung, *Unbound Feet,* pp. 7–8, 25, 27.

4. Edward C. Lydon, "The Anti Chinese Movement in Santa Cruz County, California: 1859–1900," in *The Life, Influence and Role of the Chinese in the United*

States, 1776–1960, ed. Chinese Historical Society of America (San Francisco: Chinese Historical Society of America, 1976) p. 234.

5. Ibid., pp. 227, 228, 231, 234, 240.

6. Quoted in Monroy, *Thrown Among Strangers,* pp. 201–2.

7. On Mexicans, see Ibid., pp. 201–3, and Pitt, *The Decline of the Californios,* pp. 60–64. For the Chinese, see Tsai, *The Chinese Experience in America,* p. 13; Melendy, *The Oriental Americans,* p. 43; Chan, *Bittersweet Soil,* p. 58; Chinn, Lai, and Choy, *A History of the Chinese in California,* pp. 24, 31; Knoll, *Becoming Americans,* p. 16; Li-hua Yu, "Chinese Immigration into Idaho" (Ph.D. diss., Bowling Green State University, 1991), pp. 238–40; Gary Be Dunnah, *A History of the Chinese in Nevada, 1855–1904* (San Francisco: R & E Research Associates, 1973), pp. 9–13, 17–18, chapter 9; Shi Xu, "The Image of the Chinese in the Rocky Mountain Region, 1855–1882" (Ph.D. diss., Brigham Young University, 1996), pp. 93–97.

8. Monroy, *Thrown Among Strangers,* pp. 203–4; Pitt, *The Decline of the Californios,* pp. 86–102; David Montejano, *Anglos and Mexicans in the Making of Texas, 1836–1986* (Austin: University of Texas Press, 1987), pp. 51–52, 60, 312–15; Camarillo, *Chicanos in a Changing Society,* pp. 114–15; Sheridan, *Los Tucsonenses,* pp. 72–73.

9. Quoted in Arnoldo De León, *The Tejano Community, 1836–1900* (Albuquerque: University of New Mexico Press, 1982), p. 62.

10. Sylvester Mowry, *Arizona and Sonora: The Geography, History, and Resources of the Silver Region of North America* (New York: Arno Press, 1973), pp. 234–35.

11. Sheridan, *Los Tucsonenses,* p. 35.

12. Mario Barrera, *Race and Class in the Southwest: A Theory of Racial Inequality* (Notre Dame, Ind.: University of Notre Dame Press, 1979), p. 41; Sheridan, *Los Tucsonenses,* p. 35.

13. Daniels, *Pioneer Urbanites,* pp. 33–34.

14. Ibid., pp. 35–38.

15. Claire O'Brien, "'With One Mighty Pull': Interracial Town Boosting in Nicodemus, Kansas," *Great Plains Quarterly* 16 (spring 1996): 118, 127.

16. Zhu, *Chinaman's Chance,* pp. 65, 160, 162, 163, 185.

17. Quoted in Larry D. Quinn, "'Chink Chink Chinaman': The Beginning of Nativism in Montana," *Pacific Northwest Quarterly* 58 (April 1987): 86.

18. Melendy, *The Oriental Americans,* pp. 46–48; Chen, *The Chinese in America,* pp. 69, 70, 71; Tsai, *The Chinese Experience in America,* p. 16; Chinn, Lai, and Choy, *A History of the Chinese in California,* pp. 44–46.

19. Tsai, *The Chinese Experience in America,* p. 17; Mark and Chih, *A Place Called Chinese America,* p. 10; Chinn, Lai, and Choy, *A History of the Chinese in California,* p. 45.

20. Quoted in Melendy, *The Oriental Americans,* p. 48.

21. Chinn, Lai, and Choy, *A History of the Chinese in California,* p. 45; Chen, *The Chinese of America,* pp. 69, 70–71; Tsai, *The Chinese Experience in America,* p. 1; Stephen E. Ambrose, *Nothing Like it in the World: The Men Who Built the Transcontinental Railroad, 1863–1869* (New York: Simon and Schuster, 2000).

22. Chen, *The Chinese of America,* p. 76; Tsai, *The Chinese Experience in America,* pp. 18–19; Chinn, Lai, and Choy, *A History of the Chinese in California,* pp. 46, 47; A. Dudley Gardner, "Chinese Emigrants in Southwest Wyoming, 1868–1885," *Annals of Wyoming* 63 (fall 1991): 140; Christopher H. Edson, *The Chinese in Eastern Oregon, 1860–1890* (San Francisco: R & E Research Associates, 1974), p. 58; Mark and Chih, *A Place Called Chinese America,* p. 20.

23. Savage, *Blacks in the West,* pp. 7–8; Cox, *Blacks in Topeka, Kansas,* pp. 17–18; Richard B. Sheridan, "From Slavery in Missouri to Freedom in Kansas: The Influx of the Black Fugitives and Contrabands into Kansas, 1854–1865," *Kansas History* 12 (spring 1989): 43, 44, 46; Katz, *The Black West,* p. 114; Taylor, *In Search of the Racial Frontier,* p. 96.

24. Monroe Lee Billington, *New Mexico's Buffalo Soldiers, 1866–1900* (Niwot: University Press of Colorado, 1991), p. xi; Bringhurst, "The 'Descendants of Ham' in Zion," p. 314; Arlen Fowler, *The Black Infantry in the West, 1869–1891* (Westport, Conn.: Greenwood Press, 1971), pp. 12–13; Thomas D. Philips, "The Black Regulars," in *The West of the American People,* ed. Allan G. Bogue et al. (Itasca, Ill.: F. E. Peabody Publishers, Inc., 1970), pp. 138–39; Sheridan, "From Slavery in Missouri to Freedom in Kansas," pp. 43, 44, 46; Bernson and Eggers, "Black People in South Dakota History," p. 246.

25. Bernson and Eggers, "Black People in South Dakota History," p. 246; Phillips, "The Black Regulars," pp. 138–39; Katz, *The Black West,* pp. 204, 206, 208, 234–36; Savage, *Blacks in the West,* pp. 60–61, 54–55; Billington, *New Mexico Buffalo Soldiers,* pp. 10–12, 26, 31; Fowler, *Black Infantry in the West,* pp. 51–52, 23–25; Dale T. Shoenberger, "The Black Man in the American West," *Negro History Bulletin* 32 (March 1969): p. 10, passim; Taylor, *In Search of the Racial Frontier,* pp. 170–71, 172–73; Coleman, "History of Blacks in Utah," pp. 112–20.

26. Frank N. Schubert, *Black Valor: Buffalo Soldiers and the Medal of Honor, 1870–1898* (Wilmington, Del.: SR Books, 1997), pp. xi, 79–83.

27. Carey McWilliams, *North From Mexico: The Spanish-Speaking People of*

the United States (New York: Greenwood Press, 1968), p. 136; Gómez-Quiñones, *Mexican American Labor,* pp. 48–49; Pitt, *The Decline of the Californios,* pp. 255–56.

28. McWilliams, *North From Mexico,* pp. 137–38.

29. Ibid., p. 140.

30. Frederick Law Olmsted, *A Journey through Texas* (New York: Burt Franklin, 1969), p. 160.

31. Erasmo Gamboa, "The Mexican Pack System of Transportation in the Pacific Northwest and British Columbia," *Journal of the West* 29 (January 1990): 16–27.

32. De León, *The Tejano Community,* pp. 89, 90; Gómez-Quiñones, *Mexican American Labor,* p. 50; M. L. Miranda, *A History of Hispanics in Southern Nevada* (Reno: University of Nevada Press, 1997), p. 47.

33. Zhu, *Chinaman's Chance,* p. 114.

34. Montejano, *Anglos and Mexicans in the Making of Texas,* pp. 80–83. Quote is from Tom Lea, *The King Ranch,* 2 vols. (Boston: Little, Brown and Company, 1957), 2:482–83, 567.

35. Chris Friday, *Organizing Asian American Labor: The Pacific Coast Canned-Salmon Industry, 1870–1942* (Philadelphia: Temple University Press, 1994), pp. 26, 28.

Chapter 4

1. De León, *The Tejano Community,* p. 151. See further Robert T. Trotter II and Juan Antonio Chavira, *Curanderismo: Mexican American Folk Healing* (Athens: University of Georgia Press, 1981).

2. Manuel G. Gonzales, *The Hispanic Elite in the Southwest* (El Paso: University of Texas at El Paso Press, 1989); Savage, *Blacks in the West,* pp 120–23, 128; Rusco, *"Good Time Coming?"* p. 166; Taylor, *In Search of the Racial Frontier,* pp. 197–98; Daniels, *Pioneer Urbanites,* p. 45; Chan, *Bittersweet Soil,* pp. 71, 149–54, 193–94, 231, 264, and chapter 6; Zhu, *Chinaman's Chance,* pp. 117, 144–45; June Mei, "Socio-Economic Developments among the Chinese in San Francisco, 1848–1906," in *Labor Immigration Under Capitalism: Asian Workers in the United States Before World War II,* ed. Lucie Cheng and Edna Bonacich (Berkeley: University of California Press, 1984), p. 382; Chin-Yu Chen, "San Francisco's Chinatown: A Socio-Economic and Cultural History, 1850–1882" (Ph.D. diss., University of Idaho, 1992), pp. 92–95; Yu, "Chinese Immigrants in Idaho," pp. 111–14, 123–25; Edward J. M. Rhoads, "Chinese in Texas," *Southwestern Historical Quarterly* 81 (July 1977): 12; Paul Ong, "An Ethnic Trade: The Chinese Laundries in Early California," *Journal of Ethnic Studies* 8 (winter 1981): 95, 101–2; Liestman, "The Chinese in the Black Hills," pp. 76–77; Sylvia Sun Minnick, *Samfow: The*

San Joaquin Chinese Legacy (Fresno, Calif: Panorama West Publishing, 1988), pp. 143–48.

3. Roger D. Hardaway, "African-American Women on the Western Frontier," *Negro History Bulletin* 60 (January–March 1997): 10.

4. Sandra L. Stephens, "The Women of the Amador Family, 1860–1940," in *New Mexico Women: Intercultural Perspectives,* ed. Joan M. Jensen and Darlis Miller (Albuquerque: University of New Mexico Press, 1986).

5. Benson Tong, *Unsubmissive Women: Chinese Prostitutes in Nineteenth Century San Francisco* (Norman: University of Oklahoma Press, 1994), p. 17.

6. Daniels, *Pioneer Urbanites,* p. 132; Cox, *Blacks in Topeka, Kansas,* pp. 89–90; Woods, *A Black Odyssey,* pp. 45, 46, 94. On Dodge City, Kansas, see C. Robert Haywood, "'No Less a Man': Blacks in Cow Town Dodge City, 1876–1886," *Western Historical Quarterly* 19 (May 1988): 165.

7. Daniels, *Pioneer Urbanites,* pp. 126, 135–37; Cox, *Blacks in Topeka, Kansas,* pp. 89–90; Woods, *A Black Odyssey,* pp. 45, 94, 71.

8. Daniels, *Pioneer Urbanites,* pp. 128–29, 131–32.

9. Camarillo, *Chicanos in a Changing Society,* pp. 69, 70; Sheridan, *Los Tucsonenses,* pp. 47, 107; De León, *The Tejano Community,* pp. xvi, 174–75, 185, 190.

10. F. Arturo Rosales, "'Fantasy Heritage' Re-examined: Race and Class in the Writings of the Bandini Family Authors and Other Californios, 1825–1965," in *Rediscovering the U.S. Hispanic Literary Heritage,* vol. 2, ed. Erlinda Gonzales-Berry and Chuck Tatum (Houston, Tex.: Arte Público Press, 1996) pp. 84, 95, 100–101; Sheridan, *Los Tucsonenses,* p. 107; John Chávez, *The Lost Land: The Chicano Image of the Southwest* (Albuquerque: University of New Mexico Press, 1984).

11. Gómez-Quiñones, *Mexican American Labor,* p. 41.

12. Raymond Lou, "The Chinese American Community of Los Angeles, 1870–1900: A Case Study of Resistance, Organization, and Participation" (Ph.D. diss., University of California at Irvine, 1982), pp. 40–41.

13. Liestman, "The Chinese in the Black Hills," p. 74; Melendy, *The Oriental Americans,* p. 12; Chinn, Lai, and Choy, *History of the Chinese in California,* p. 12.

14. Chan, "Exclusion of Chinese Women," pp. 95, 97–139.

15. David Beesley, "From Chinese to Chinese Americans: Chinese Women and Families in Sierra Nevada Towns," *California History* 67 (September 1988): 170.

16. Lyman, *The Asian in the West*, p. 18; Judy Yung, *Chinese Women of America: A Pictorial History* (Seattle: University of Washington Press, 1986), p. 118.

17. Hing, *Making and Remaking Asian America Through Immigration Policy*, p. 46.

18. Hui-Chen Wang Liu, *The Traditional Chinese Clan Rules* (Locust Valley, N.Y.: J. J. Augustin Publishers, 1959), pp. 1–3; Maurice Freedman, "The Family in China, Past and Present," *Pacific Affairs* (winter 1961–1962): 327; Xia, "The Sojourner Myth and Chinese Immigrants," pp. 35–36.

19. Freedman, "The Family in China," p. 328; Ronald Takaki, *A Different Mirror: A History of Multicultural America* (Boston: Little, Brown and Company, 1993), pp. 209–10.

20. Yung, *Unbound Feet*, pp. 6, 7, 18–20, 24 25, 41.

21. Ibid., pp. 29, 41; Beesley, "From Chinese to Chinese Americans," p. 171; Liestman, "Chinese in the Black Hills," p. 81.

22. Yung, *Unbound Feet*, pp. 27–30; Johnson, *Roaring Camp*, pp. 298–99; Mark and Chih, *A Place Called Chinese America*, pp. 62 63; Beesley, "From Chinese to Chinese Americans," p. 171; Tong, *Unsubmissive Women*, chapter 2, Lou, "The Chinese American Community of Los Angeles," pp. 288–302; Chin-Yu Chen, "San Francisco's Chinatown," pp. 71–76.

23. Lucie Cheng, "Free, Indentured, Enslaved: Chinese Prostitutes in Nineteenth Century America," in Cheng and Bonacich, *Labor Immigration Under Capitalism*, pp. 402–34.

24. Tong, *Unsubmissive Women*, pp. 145–46, 173–74, 176, 190, 194–95.

25. Ibid., pp. 6–9, 12; Yung, *Unbound Feet*, pp. 33–34.

26. Quoted in Dan Caldwell, "The Negroization of the Chinese Stereotype in California," *Southern California Quarterly* 53 (1971): 128.

27. Charles L. Kenner, *Buffalo Soldiers and Officers of the Ninth Cavalry, 1867–1898* (Norman: University of Oklahoma Press, 1999), pp. 251–53.

28. Tong, *Unsubmissive Women*, pp. 177–87.

29. Yung, *Unbound Feet*, pp. 43–44.

30. Yu, "Chinese Immigrants in Idaho," pp. 205–6, 212; Chan, *Bittersweet Soil*, pp. 390–91.

31. Yung, *Unbound Feet*, p. 41; Mark and Chih, *A Place Called Chinese America*, pp. 62–63; Beesley, "From Chinese to Chinese Americans," pp. 170, 174; Sucheng Chan, "The Exclusion of Chinese Women, 1870–1943," pp. 114–15, 138–39; Lou, "The Chinese American Community of Los Angeles," pp. 303–20; Tong, *Unsubmissive Women*, chapter 6.

32. Lou, "The Chinese American Community of Los Angeles," pp. 285, 326–28; Yung, *Unbound Feet,* pp. 45–46.

33. Yu, "Chinese Immigrants in Idaho," pp. 30–37, 39, 202–3, 206–7; Tong, *Unsubmissive Women,* pp. 169–71.

34. Richard Griswold del Castillo, *The Los Angeles Barrio, 1850–1890: A Social History* (Berkeley: University of California Press, 1980), pp. 74–75; Richard Griswold del Castillo, *La Familia: Chicano Families in the Urban Southwest, 1848 to the Present* (Notre Dame, Ind.: University of Notre Dame Press, 1984), pp. 67, 68, 69; Sheridan, *Los Tucsonenses,* p. 146; Pitt, *The Decline of the Californios,* pp. 125, 268; Darlis Miller, "Cross-Cultural Marriages in the Southwest: The New Mexico Experience, 1846–1900," in Jensen and Miller, *New Mexico Women,* pp. 97–101.

35. Montejano, *Anglos and Mexicans in the Making of Texas,* pp. 34, 37; Gonzales, *The Hispanic Elite,* p. 25.

36. Miller, "Cross-Cultural Marriages," pp. 110–11.

37. Barry A. Crouch, "Black Dreams and White Justice," *Prologue* 6 (winter 1974): 263.

Chapter 5

1. Liestman, "The Chinese in the Black Hills," p. 79; Barth, *Bitter Strength,* pp. 123–24; Melendy, *The Oriental Americans,* p. 77; Chen, *The Chinese of America,* p. 120; Yu, "Chinese Immigrants in Idaho," pp. 164, 168–69.

2. Sheridan, *Los Tucsonenses,* pp. 151, 152; Pitt, *The Decline of the Californios,* p. 215; Gómez-Quiñones, *Mexican American Labor,* p. 43.

3. Paul Horgan, *Lamy of Santa Fe: His Life and Times* (New York: Farrar, Straus and Giroux, 1975), pp. 129–30, 240–44, 249–51, 256, 353; McWilliams, *North From Mexico,* p. 118.

4. Quoted in Rusco, *"Good Time Coming?"* p. 281.

5. Phillips, "Black Regulars," p. 142; Fowler, *The Black Infantry,* pp. 92–93, quote from pp. 96–97.

6. Daniels, *Pioneer Urbanites,* p. 19; Irving G. Hendrick, *The Education of Non-whites in California, 1849–1970* (San Francisco: R & E Research Associates, 1977), pp. 9–10.

7. Savage, *Blacks in the West,* pp. 178–79.

8. Rosaura Sánchez, *Telling Identities: The California Testimonios* (Minneapolis: University of Minnesota Press, 1995), p. ix.

9. Jesús F. de la Teja, ed., *A Revolution Remembered: The Memoirs and*

Selected Correspondence of Juan N. Seguín (Austin, Tex.: State House Press, 1991), p. vii; David R. McDonald and Timothy M. Matovina, eds., *Defending Mexican Valor in Texas: José Antonio Navarro's Historical Writing, 1853–1857* (Austin, Tex.: State House Press, 1995), pp. 11–12, 21–26.

10. Sánchez, *Telling Identities,* pp. ix, x, 6.

11. Ibid., pp. 3, 276–79; Génaro Padilla, "Recovering Mexican American Autobiography," in *Recovering the U.S. Hispanic Literary Heritage,* vol. 1., ed. Ramón Gutiérrez and Génaro Padilla (Houston: Arte Público Press, 1993), pp. 167–70.

12. Savage, *Blacks in the West,* pp. 128–29; Cox, *Blacks in Topeka, Kansas,* p. 83; Woods, *Black Odyssey,* pp. 59–60; Rusco, *"Good Time Coming?"* p. 71; J. William Snorgrass, "The Black Press in the San Francisco Bay Area, 1856–1900," *California History* 60 (winter 1981–1982): 306–8.

13. Katz, *The Black West,* pp. 195–96.

14. Cox, *Blacks in Topeka, Kansas,* pp. 83–84; Rusco, *"Good Time Coming?"* pp. 71, 48; Daniels, *Pioneer Urbanites,* pp. 114–15; Taylor, *In Search of the Racial Frontier,* pp. 93–94, 197.

15. De León, *The Tejano Community,* pp. 144–45, 183; Reed Anderson, "Early Secular Theatre in New Mexico," in *Pasó por Aquí: Critical Essays on the New Mexican Literary Tradition, 1542–1988,* ed. Erlinda Gonzales-Berry (Albuquerque: University of New Mexico Press, 1989), pp. 104–24; Nick Kanellos, *A History of the Hispanic Theatre in the United States: Origins to 1940* (Austin: University of Texas Press, 1990), pp. 2, 5; Sheridan, *Los Tucsonenses,* pp. 199, 200; Griswold del Castillo, *The Los Angeles Barrio,* p. 73.

16. Kanellos, *History of the Hispanic Theatre,* pp. 1–16; Rosemary Gipson, "The Mexican Performers: Pioneer Theatre Artists of Tucson," *Journal of Arizona History* 13 (winter 1972): 239, 246.

17. Savage, *Blacks in the West,* p. 127.

18. Fowler, *The Black Infantry,* pp. 57–58, 63.

19. Sheridan, "From Slavery in Missouri to Freedom in Kansas," p. 40; Lapp, *Blacks in Gold Rush California,* p. 191; Howard H. Bell, "Negroes in California, 1849–1859," *Phylon* 28 (1967): 154; Savage, *Blacks in the West,* pp. 186–87.

20. Daniels, *Frontier Urbanites,* p. 120; Savage, *Blacks in the West,* p. 186; Rusco, *"Good Time Coming?"* p. 176; Richard, "Unwelcomed Settlers," pp. 181–84; McLagan, *A Peculiar Paradise,* p. 91; Sheridan, "From Slavery in Missouri to Freedom in Kansas," p. 40. On the function and symbolism of popular festivals, see Ellen M. Litwicki, "'Our Hearts Burn with Ardent Love for Two Countries':

Ethnicity and Assimilation at Chicago Holiday Celebrations," *Journal of American Ethnic History* 19 (spring 2000).

21. Richard, "Unwelcomed Settlers," pp. 183–84; MacLagan, *A Peculiar Paradise*, pp. 91–92; Daniels, *Pioneer Urbanites*, p. 121.

22. Yu, "Chinese Immigrants in Idaho," p. 213.

23. Chen, *The Chinese of America*, pp. 120–21; Barth, *Bitter Strength*, pp. 121–22; Sandy Lydon, *Chinese Gold: The Chinese in the Monterey Bay Region* (Capitola, Calif.: Capitola Book Co., 1985), pp. 256–58; Tsai, *The Chinese Experience in America*, p. 36; Liestman, "The Chinese in the Black Hills," p. 80; Magnaghi, "Virginia City's Chinese Community, 1860–1880," p. 142; Minnick, *Samfow*, pp. 100–103; Yu, "Chinese Immigrants in Idaho," pp. 213–14, 219, 220.

24. Chen, *The Chinese of America*, p. 20; Barth, *Bitter Strength*, p. 122; Yu, "Chinese Immigrants in Idaho," pp. 213–14, 225; Tsai, *The Chinese Experience in America*, p. 36; Magnaghi, "Virginia City's Chinese Community," p. 142; Yu, "Chinese Immigrants in Idaho," pp. 213–14, 225.

25. Lydon, *Chinese Gold*, pp. 261–66; Yu, "Chinese Immigrants in Idaho," pp. 222–24; Liestman, "The Chinese in the Black Hills," p. 79; Zhu, *Chinaman's Chance*, pp. 161–62.

26. Liestman, "The Chinese in the Black Hills," p. 77; Magnaghi, "Virginia City's Chinese Community," p. 139; Yu, "Chinese Immigrants in Idaho," p. 198; Chin-Yu Chen, "San Francisco's Chinatown," p. 76.

27. Yu, "Chinese Immigrants in Idaho," p. 198; Florence D. Lister and Robert H. Lister, *The Chinese of Early Tucson: Historic Archaeology from the Tucson Urban Renewal Project* (Tucson: University of Arizona Press, 1989), p. 69; Liestman, "The Chinese in the Black Hills," p. 81.

28. Chen, *The Chinese of America*, p. 61; Tsai, *The Chinese Experience in America*, p. 38; Lou, "The Chinese American Community of Los Angeles," p. 206; Yu, "Chinese Immigrants in Idaho," p. 199; Zhu, *Chinaman's Chance*, p. 27; Raymond Lou, "Community Resistance of Los Angeles Chinese Americans, 1870–1900: A Case Study of Gaming," in *The Chinese American Experience: Papers from the Second National Conference on Chinese American Studies*, ed. Genny Lim (San Francisco: The Chinese Historical Society of America and the Chinese Cultural Foundation of San Francisco, 1984), pp. 160–66. In part because of its "immorality," but also its tendency to attract criminal elements, the city government in Los Angeles passed ordinances during the 1880s shutting down Fan-Tan establishments, but the game persisted surreptitiously. Ibid., pp. 164, 166.

29. Yu, "Chinese Immigrants in Idaho," pp. 199, 200; Zhu, *Chinaman's Chance*, p. 27; Lou, "Community Resistance of Los Angeles Chinese Americans," pp. 160–61.

30. Lisbeth Haas, *Conquests and Historical Identities in California, 1769–1936* (Berkeley: University of California Press, 1995), pp. 116, 118; Doris Meyer, *Speaking for Themselves: Neo-Mexicano Cultural Identity and the Spanish Language Press, 1880–1920* (Albuquerque: University of New Mexico Press, 1996), pp. 20, 22.

31. Gómez-Quiñones, *Mexican American Labor*, p. 42; De León, *The Tejano Community*, pp. 156–57, 160–61, 164, 169.

32. Paul Wright, "Population Patterns in Presidio County in 1880: Evidence from the Census," *Journal of Big Bend Studies* 7 (January 1995): 181–201.

33. Wesley Woo, "Chinese Protestants in the San Francisco Bay Area," in Chan, *Entry Denied*, pp. 225–26, 228–29, 233–34.

34. Magnaghi, "Virginia City's Chinese Community," p. 132; Zhu, *Chinaman's Chance*, p. 23; Lou, "Chinese American Community of Los Angeles," p. 130; Lister and Lister, *The Chinese of Early Tucson*, p. 61; Chinn, Lai, and Choy, *History of the Chinese in California*, p. 72; Chen, *The Chinese of America*, p. 119; Liestman, "The Chinese of the Black Hills," p. 78; Stanford M. Lyman, "The Chinese Diaspora in America, 1850–1943," in Chinese Historical Society of America, *The Life, Influence, and Role of the Chinese* (San Francisco: Chinese Historical Society of America, 1976), pp. 132–33.

35. Zhu, *Chinaman's Chance*, pp. 66–67.

36. Quoted in Camarillo, *Chicanos in a Changing Society*, p. 62.

37. De León, *The Tejano Community*, p 176.

38. John Hope Franklin and Alfred A. Moss, Jr., *From Slavery to Freedom: A History of Negro Americans*, 8th ed. (New York: Alfred A. Knopf, 2000), pp. 114–16.

39. Daniels, *Pioneer Urbanites*, pp. 112–13, 118–19; Philip M. Montesano, "San Francisco's Black Churches in the Early 1860s: Political Pressure Group," *California Historical Quarterly* 52 (summer 1973): 145; Cox, *Blacks in Topeka, Kansas*, p. 31; Coray, "African Americans in Nevada," pp. 242, 255; Rusco, "Good Time Coming?" pp. 178–79.

40. Savage, *Blacks in the West*, pp. 127–28.

Epilogue

1. Alwyn Barr, "Black Legislators of Reconstruction Texas," *Civil War History: A Journal of the Middle Period* 32 (December 1986), 340–51. See further,

Barry A. Crouch, "Hesitant Recognition: Texas Black Politicians, 1865–1900," *East Texas State Historical Journal* 31, no. 1 (1993): 41–58.

2. Lydon, *Chinese Gold,* pp. 24, 67–70.

3. Chan, *Bittersweet Soil,* pp. 213, 222.

4. Griswold del Castillo, *La Familia,* pp. 81, 86–87.

5. Meyer, *Speaking for Themselves,* pp. 191–205, 252 note 47.

BIBLIOGRAPHY

Books:

Almaguer, Tomás. *Racial Fault Lines: The Historical Origins of White Supremacy in California*. Berkeley: University of California Press, 1994.

Ambrose, Stephen E. *Nothing Like It in the World: The Men Who Built the Transcontinental Railroad, 1863–1869*. New York: Simon and Schuster, 2000.

Athearn, Robert G. *In Search of Canaan: Black Migration to Kansas, 1879–1880*. Lawrence: Regents Press of Kansas, 1978.

Barrera, Mario. *Race and Class in the Southwest: A Theory of Racial Inequality*. Notre Dame, Ind.: University of Notre Dame Press, 1979.

Barth, Gunther. *Bitter Strength: A History of Chinese in the U.S., 1850–1870*. Cambridge, Mass.: Harvard University Press, 1964.

Beasley, Delilah L. *The Negro Trail Blazers of California*. Los Angeles: Times Mirror Printing and Binding House, 1919.

Billington, Monroe Lee. *New Mexico's Buffalo Soldiers, 1866–1900*. Niwot: University Press of Colorado, 1991.

Billington, Ray Allen. *America's Frontier Heritage*. Albuquerque: University of New Mexico Press, 1974.

Bogue, Allan G., et al., eds. *The West of the American People*. Itasca, Ill.: F. E. Peabody Publishers, Inc., 1970.

Bond, J. Max. *The Negro in Los Angeles*. San Francisco: R & E Research Associates, 1972.

Bringhurst, Newell G. *Saints, Slaves, and Blacks: The Changing Place of Black People Within Mormonism*. Westport, Conn.: Greenwood Press, 1981.

Camarillo, Albert. *Chicanos in a Changing Society: From Mexican Pueblos to American Barrios in Santa Barbara and Southern California*. Cambridge: Harvard University Press, 1979.

Campa, Arthur L. *Hispanic Culture in the Southwest*. Norman: University of Oklahoma Press, 1979.

Chan, Sucheng. *Asian Americans: An Interpretive History*. Boston: Twayne Publishers, 1991.

———. *Asian Californians*. San Francisco: MTL/Boyd and Fraser, 1991.

———. *Entry Denied: Exclusion and the Chinese Community in America, 1882–1943*. Philadelphia: Temple University Press, 1991.

————. *This Bittersweet Soil: The Chinese in California Agriculture, 1860–1910.* Berkeley: University of California Press, 1986.

Chan, Sucheng, et al., eds. *Peoples of Color in the American West.* Lexington, Mass: D. C. Heath and Co., 1994.

Chávez, John. *The Lost Land: The Chicano Image of the Southwest.* Albuquerque: University of New Mexico Press, 1984.

Chen, Jack. *The Chinese of America: From the Beginnings to the Present.* San Francisco: Harper and Row, 1980.

Cheng, Lucie, and Edna Bonacich, eds. *Labor Immigration under Capitalism: Asian Workers in the U.S. before World War II.* Berkeley: University of California Press, 1984.

Chin, Doug, and Art Chin. *Up Hill: The Settlement and Diffusion of the Chinese in Seattle, Washington.* Seattle: Shorey Original Publications, 1973.

Chinese Historical Society of America. *The Life, Influence, and Role of the Chinese in the United States, 1776–1960.* San Francisco: Chinese Historical Society of America, 1976.

Chinn, Thomas W. *Bridging the Pacific: San Francisco's Chinatown and Its People.* San Francisco: Chinese Historical Society of America, 1989.

Chinn, Thomas W., H. Mark Lai, and Philip P. Choy, eds. *A History of the Chinese in California: A Syllabus.* San Francisco: Chinese Historical Society of America, 1969.

Corwin, Arthur, ed. *Immigrants—and Immigrants: Perspectives on Labor Migration to the United States.* Westport, Conn.: Greenwood Press, 1978.

Cox, Thomas Cooper. *Blacks in Topeka, Kansas, 1865–1915: Social History.* Baton Rouge: Louisiana State University Press, 1982.

Daniels, Douglas Henry. *Pioneer Urbanites: A Social and Cultural History of Black San Francisco.* Berkeley: University of California Press, 1990.

De la Teja, Jesús F., ed. *A Revolution Remembered: The Memoirs and Selective Correspondence of Juan N. Seguín.* Austin, Tex.: State House Press, 1991.

De León, Arnoldo. *The Mexican Image in Nineteenth Century Texas.* Boston: American Press, 1982.

————. *They Called Them Greasers: Anglo Attitudes Toward Mexicans in Texas, 1821–1900.* Austin: University of Texas Press, 1983.

————. *The Tejano Community, 1836–1900.* Albuquerque: University of New Mexico Press, 1982.

Driver, Harold E. *Indians of North America.* Chicago: University of Chicago Press, 1961.

Dunnah, Gary Be. *A History of the Chinese in Nevada, 1855–1904*. San Francisco: R & E Research Associates, 1973

Edson, Christopher H. *The Chinese in Eastern Oregon, 1860–1890*. San Francisco: R & E Research Associates, 1974.

Etulain, Richard W. *Writing Western History: Essays on Major Western Historians*. Albuquerque: University of New Mexico Press, 1991.

Fowler, Arlen. *The Black Infantry in the West, 1869–1891*. Westport, Conn.: Greenwood Press, 1971.

Franklin, John Hope, and Alfred A. Moss, Jr. *From Slavery to Freedom: A History of Negro Americans*. 8th ed. New York: Alfred A. Knopf, 2000.

Friday, Chris. *Organizing Asian American Laborers: The Pacific Coast Canned-Salmon Industry, 1870–1942*. Philadelphia: Temple University Press, 1994.

Gómez-Quiñones, Juan. *Mexican American Labor, 1790–1990*. Albuquerque: University of New Mexico Press, 1994.

Gonzales-Berry, Erlinda, ed. *Pasó Por Aquí: Critical Essays on the New Mexico Literary Tradition*. Albuquerque: University of New Mexico Press, 1989.

Gonzales-Berry, Erlinda, and David Maciel, eds. *The Contested Homeland: A Chicano History of New Mexico, 1546–1988*. Albuquerque: University of New Mexico Press, 2000.

Gonzales-Berry, Erlinda, and Chuck Tatum. *Recovering the Hispanic Literary Heritage*, vol. 2. Houston, Tex.: Arte Público Press, 1996.

Gonzales, Manuel. *The Hispanic Elite of the Southwest*. El Paso: University of Texas at El Paso, 1989.

Goode, Kenneth G. *California's Black Pioneers: A Brief Historical Survey*. Santa Barbara, Calif.: McNally and Loftin, 1974.

Griswold del Castillo, Richard. *La Familia: Chicano Families in the Urban Southwest, 1848 to the Present*. Notre Dame, Ind.: University of Notre Dame Press, 1984.

———. *The Los Angeles Barrio, 1850–1890: A Social History*. Berkeley: University of California Press, 1980.

Gutiérrez, Ramón, and Génaro Padilla, eds. *Recovering the United States Hispanic Literary Heritage*, vol. 1. Houston, Tex.: Arte Público Press, 1993.

Haas, Lisbeth. *Conquests and Historical Identities in California, 1769–1936*. Berkeley: University of California Press, 1995.

Halseth, James A., and Bruce A. Glasrud, eds. *The Northwest Mosaic: Minority Conflict in the Pacific Northwest*. Boulder, Colo.: Pruett Publishing Co., 1977.

Hendrick, Irving G. *The Education of Non-Whites in California, 1849–1970*. San Francisco: R & E Research Associates, 1977.

Hing, Bill Ong. *Making and Remaking Asian America Through Immigration Policy,
1850–1990.* Stanford, Calif.: Stanford University Press, 1993.

Horgan, Paul. *Lamy of Santa Fe: His Life and Times.* New York: Farrar, Straus,
and Giroux, 1975.

Hunt, Michael H. *The Making of a Special Relationship: The United States and
China to 1914.* New York: Columbia University Press, 1983.

Huson, Howard. *Refugio: A Comprehensive History of Refugio County from Aboriginal
Times to 1955.* 2 vols. Woodsboro, Tex.: The Rooke Foundation, 1956.

Jacobs, Wilbur R. *On Turner's Trail: 100 Years of Writing Western History.*
Lawrence: University Press of Kansas, 1994.

Jensen, Joan, and Darlis Miller, eds. *New Mexico Women: Intercultural Perspectives.*
Albuquerque: University of New Mexico Press, 1986.

Johnson, Susan Lee. *Roaring Camp: The Social World of the California Gold Rush.*
New York: W. W. Norton & Company, 2000.

Kanellos, Nick. *A History of the Hispanic Theatre in the United States: Origins to
1940.* Austin: University of Texas Press, 1990.

Katz, William L. *The Black West.* New York: Doubleday, 1973.

Kenner, Charles L. *Buffalo Soldiers and Officers of the Ninth Cavalry, 1867–1898.*
Norman: University of Oklahoma Press, 1999.

King, S. W. *Chinese of American Life: Some Aspects of Their History, Status,
Problems and Contributions.* Seattle: University of Washington Press, 1962.

Knoll, Tricia. *Becoming Americans: Asian Sojourners, Immigrants, and Refugees
in the Western United States.* Portland: Coast-to-Coast Books, 1982.

Lapp, Rudolph M. *Blacks in Gold Rush California.* New Haven: Yale University
Press, 1977.

Lea, Tom. *The King Ranch.* 2 vols. Boston: Little, Brown and Company, 1957.

Lim, Genny, ed. *The Chinese American Experience.* San Francisco: Chinese
Historical Society of America and the Chinese Cultural Center, 1984.

Limerick, Patricia. *The Legacy of Conquest: The Unbroken Past of the American
West.* New York: Norton, 1988.

Limerick, Patricia, et al. *Trails: Towards a New Western History.* Lawrence:
University Press of Kansas, 1991.

Lister, Florence, and Robert H. Lister. *The Chinese of Early Tucson: Historic
Archaeology from the Tucson Urban Renewal Project.* Tucson: University of
Arizona Press, 1989.

Liu, Hui-Chen Wang. *The Traditional Chinese Clan Rules.* Locust Valley, N.Y.:
J. J. Augustin Publishers, 1959.

Low, Victor. *The Unimpressible Race: A Century of Educational Struggle by the Chinese in San Francisco.* San Francisco: East/West Publishing Co., 1982.

Lydon, Sandy. *Chinese Gold: The Chinese in the Monterey Bay Region.* Capitola, Calif.: Capitola Book Co., 1985.

Lyman, Stanford M. *The Asian in the West.* Reno: Desert Research Institute, University of Nevada, 1970.

Malone, Michael P., ed. *Historians and the American West.* Lincoln: University of Nebraska Press, 1983.

Mark, Diane Mei Lin, and Ginger Chih. *A Place Called Chinese America.* Dubuque, Iowa: Kendall/Hunt, 1982.

McClain, Charles J. *In Search of Equality: The Chinese Struggle Against Discrimination in Nineteenth Century America.* Berkeley: University of California Press, 1994.

McDonald, David, and Timothy M. Matovina, eds. *Defending Mexican Valor in Texas: José Antonio Navarro's Historical Writings, 1853–1857.* Austin, Tex.: State House Press, 1995.

McLagan, Elizabeth. *A Peculiar Paradise: A History of Blacks in Oregon, 1788–1940.* Portland, Oreg.: Georgian Press, 1980.

McLaren, John R., Hamar Foster, and Chet Orloff, eds. *Law for the Elephant, Law for the Beaver: Essays in the History of the American West.* Pasadena, Calif.: Ninth Judicial Circuit Historical Society, 1992.

McWilliams, Carey. *North From Mexico: The Spanish-Speaking Population of the United States.* New York: Greenwood Press, 1968.

Melendy, H. Brett. *The Oriental Americans.* New York: Twayne Publishers, Inc., 1972.

Meyer, Doris. *Speaking for Themselves: Neo-Mexicano Cultural Identity and the Spanish Language Press, 1880–1920.* Albuquerque: University of New Mexico Press, 1996.

Minnick, Sylvia Sun. *Samfow: The San Joaquin Chinese Legacy.* Fresno, Calif.: Panorama West Publishing, 1988.

Monroy, Douglas. *Thrown Among Strangers: The Making of Mexican Culture in Frontier California.* Berkeley: University of California Press, 1990.

Montejano, David. *Anglos and Mexicans in the Making of Texas, 1836–1986.* Austin: University of Texas Press, 1987.

Mowry, Sylvester. *Arizona and Sonora: The Geography, History and Resources of the Silver Region of North America.* New York: Arno Press, 1973.

Nash, Gerald D. *Creating the West: Historical Interpretations, 1890–1990.* Albuquerque: University of New Mexico Press, 1991.

Nostrand, Richard. *The Hispano Homeland*. Norman: University of Oklahoma Press, 1992.

Olmsted, Frederick Law. *A Journey through Texas*. New York: Burt Franklin, 1969.

Pitt, Leonard. *The Decline of the Californios: A Social History of the Spanish-Speaking Californians, 1846–1900*. Berkeley: University of California Press, 1966.

Report on Population of the United States at the Eleventh Census: 1890. Washington, D.C.: Government Printing Office, 1895.

Riley, Glenda. *Frontierswomen: The Iowa Experience*. Ames: Iowa State University Press, 1981.

Romo, Ricardo, and Raymund Paredes, eds. *New Directions in Chicano Scholarship*. La Jolla: University of California at San Diego, 1978.

Rusco, Elmer R. *"Good Time Coming?": Black Nevadans in the Nineteenth Century*. Westport, Conn.: Greenwood Press, 1975.

Sánchez, Rosaura. *Telling Identities: The California Testimonios*. Minneapolis: University of Minnesota Press, 1995.

Savage, W. Sherman. *Blacks in the West*. Westport, Conn.: Greenwood Press, 1976.

Sayler, Lucy E. *Laws Harsh as Tigers: Chinese Immigration and the Shaping of Modern Immigration Laws*. Chapel Hill: University of North Carolina Press, 1995.

Schubert, Frank N. *Black Valor: Buffalo Soldiers and the Medal of Honor, 1870–1898*. Wilmington, Del: Scholarly Resources, 1997.

Sheridan, Thomas E. *Los Tucsonenses: The Mexican Community in Tucson, 1854–1941*. Tucson: University of Arizona Press, 1986.

Smith, George G. *The Life and Times of George Foster Pierce*. Sparta, Ga.: Hancock Publishing Co., 1888.

Smurr, J. W., and K. Ross Toole, eds. *Historical Essays on Montana and the Northwest*. Helena, Montana: The Western Press, Historical Society of Montana, 1957.

Spicer, Edward M., and Raymond H. Thompson, eds. *Plural Society in the Southwest*. Albuquerque: University of New Mexico Press, 1972.

Takaki, Ronald. *A Different Mirror: A History of Multicultural America*. Boston: Little, Brown and Company, 1993.

Taylor, Quintard. *The Forging of a Black Community: Seattle's Central District from 1870 through the Civil Rights Era*. Seattle: University of Washington Press, 1994.

———. *In Search of the Racial Frontier: African Americans in the American West, 1528–1990*. New York: W. W. Norton, 1998.

Thompson, Jerry D., ed. *Juan Cortina and the Texas-Mexico Frontier, 1859–1877*. El Paso: Texas Western Press, 1994.

Tong, Benson. *Unsubmissive Women: Chinese Prostitutes in Nineteenth Century San Francisco.* Norman: University of Oklahoma Press, 1994.

Trotter II, Robert T., and Juan Antonio Chavira. *Curanderismo: Mexican American Folk Healing.* Athens: University of Georgia Press, 1981.

Tsai, Shih-Shan Henry. *The Chinese Experience in America.* Bloomington: Indiana University Press, 1986.

Weber, David J. *The Mexican Frontier, 1821–1848: The American Southwest under Mexico.* Albuquerque: University of New Mexico Press, 1982.

Weber, David J., and Jane M. Rausch, eds. *Where Cultures Meet: Frontiers in Latin American History.* Wilmington, Del.: SR Books, 1994.

Woods, Randall B. *A Black Odyssey: John Lewis Waller and the Promise of American Life, 1878–1900.* Lawrence: Regents Press of Kansas, 1981.

Wyman, Walker D., and Clifton B. Kroeber, eds. *The Frontier in Perspective.* Madison: University of Wisconsin Press, 1965.

Yung, Judy. *Unbound Feet: A Social History of Chinese Women in San Francisco.* Berkeley: University of California Press, 1995.

———. *Chinese Women of America: A Pictorial History.* Seattle: University of Washington Press, 1986.

Zhu, Liping. *A Chinaman's Chance: The Chinese in the Rocky Mountain Mining Region.* Niwot: University Press of Colorado, 1997.

Zo, Kil Young. *Chinese Emigration into the U.S., 1850–1880.* New York: Arno Press, 1978.

Articles:

Anderson, Grant K. "Deadwood's Chinatown." *South Dakota History* 5 (summer 1975).

Barr, Alwyn. "Black Legislators of Reconstruction Texas." *Civil War History: A Journal of the Middle Period* 32 (December 1986).

Beesley, David. "From Chinese to Chinese Americans: Chinese Women and Families in Sierra Nevada Towns." *California History* 67 (September 1988).

Bell, Howard H. "Negroes in California, 1849–1859." *Phylon* 28 (1967).

Bernson, Sara L., and Robert J. Eggers. "Black People in South Dakota History." *South Dakota History* 7 (summer 1977).

Berwanger, Eugene H. "Reconstruction on the Frontier: The Equal Rights Struggle in Colorado, 1865–1867." *Pacific Historical Review* 44 (August 1975).

———. "Hardin and Langston: Western Black Spokesmen of the Reconstruction Era." *Journal of Negro History* 64 (spring 1979).

————. "William J. Hardin: Colorado Spokesman for Racial Justice, 1863–1873." *Colorado Magazine* 52 (winter 1975).

Bringhurst, Newell G. "The 'Descendants of Ham' in Zion: Discrimination Against Blacks along the Shifting Mormon Frontier, 1830–1920." *Nevada Historical Society Quarterly* 24 (winter 1981).

Caldwell, Dan. "The Negroization of the Chinese Stereotype in California." *Southern California Quarterly* 53 (1971).

Carter, Gregg Lee. "Social Demography of the Chinese in Nevada, 1870–1880." *Nevada Historical Society Quarterly* 18 (summer 1975).

Chan, Loren B. "The Chinese in Nevada: A Historical Survey, 1856–1970." *Nevada Historical Society Quarterly* 25 (winter 1982).

Chandler, Robert J. "Friends in Time of Need: Republicans and Black Civil Rights in California During the Civil War Era." *Arizona and the West* 24 (winter 1982).

Chen, Yong. "The Internal Origins of Chinese Emigration to California Reconsidered." *Western Historical Quarterly* 28 (winter 1997).

Coray, Michael S. "African Americans in Nevada." *Nevada Historical Society Quarterly* 35 (winter 1992).

————. "Negro and Mulatto in the Pacific West, 1850–1860: Changing Patterns of Black Population Growth." *The Pacific Historian* 29 (winter 1985).

Crouch, Barry A. "Black Dreams and White Justice." *Prologue* 6 (winter 1974).

————. "The 'Chords of Love': Legalizing Black Marital and Family Rights in Post-War Texas." *The Journal of Negro History* 79 (fall 1994).

————. "Hesitant Recognition: Texas Black Politicians, 1865–1900." *East Texas State Historical Journal* 31, no. 1 (1993).

De Graaf, Lawrence B. "Race, Sex, and Region: Black Women in the American West, 1850–1920." *Pacific Historical Review* 49 (May 1980).

Freedman, Maurice. "The Family in China, Past and Present." *Pacific Affairs* (winter 1961–62).

Fritz, Christian G. "A Nineteenth Century 'Habeas Corpus Mill': The Chinese before the Federal Courts in California." *American Journal of Legal History* 32 (October 1988).

Gamboa, Erasmo. "The Mexican Mule Pack System of Transportation in the Pacific Northwest and British Columbia." *Journal of the West* 29 (January 1990).

Gardner, Dudley. "Chinese Emigrants in Southwest Wyoming, 1868–1885." *Annals of Wyoming* 63 (fall 1991).

Gipson, Rosemary. "The Mexican Performers: Pioneer Theatre Artists of Tucson." *Journal of Arizona History* 13 (winter 1972).

Hanchett, William. "Yankee Law and the Negro in Nevada." *Western Humanities Review* 10 (1956).

Hardaway, Roger D. "African-American Women on the Western Frontier." *Negro History Bulletin* 60 (January–March 1997).

———. "William Jefferson Hardin: Wyoming's Nineteenth Century Black Legislator." *Annals of Wyoming* 63 (winter 1991).

Hayden, Dolores. "Biddy Mason's Los Angeles, 1856–1891." *California History* 68 (fall 1984).

Haywood, C. Robert. "'No Less a Man': Blacks in Cow Town Dodge City, 1876–1886." *Western Historical Quarterly* 19 (May 1988).

Higgins, Billy D. "Negro Thought and the Exodus of 1879." *Phylon* 32 (1971).

Hogg, Thomas Clark. "Negroes and their Institutions in Oregon." *Phylon* 30 (fall 1969).

Holden, Margaret K. "Gender and Protest Ideology: Sue Ross Keenan and the Oregon Anti-Chinese Movement." *Western Legal History: The Journal of the Ninth Judicial District* (summer/fall, 1994).

Hult, Ruby El. "The Saga of George W. Bush: Unheralded Pioneer of the Northwest Territory." *Negro Digest* 11 (September 1962).

James, Ronald L. "'Why No Chinamen Are Found in Twin Falls.'" *Idaho Yesterdays* 36 (winter 1993).

Johnsen, Leigh Dana. "Equal Rights and the 'Heathen Chinee': Black Activism in San Francisco." *Western Historical Quarterly* 11 (January 1980).

Laurie, Clayton D. "'The Chinese Must Go': The U.S. Army and the Anti-Chinese Riots in Washington Territory, 1865–1886." *Pacific Northwest Quarterly* 81 (January 1990).

Liestman, Daniel. "The Chinese in the Black Hills, 1876–1932," *Journal of the West* 27 (January 1998).

———. "Utah's Chinatowns: The Development and Decline of Extinct Ethnic Enclaves." *Utah Historical Quarterly* 64 (winter 1996).

Magnaghi, Russell M. "Virginia City's Chinese Community, 1860–1880." *Nevada Historical Society Quarterly* 24 (1981).

Martínez, Oscar J. "On The Size of the Chicano Population: New Estimates, 1850–1900." *Aztlán: International Journal of Chicano Studies Research* 6 (spring 1975).

Mei, June. "Socio-Economic Origins of Emigration: Guangdong to California, 1850–1882." *Modern China* 5 (October 1979).

Montesano, Philip M. "San Francisco Black Churches in the Early 1860s: Political Pressure Group." *California Historical Quarterly* 52 (summer 1973).

Mooney, Ralph James. "Mathew Deady and the Federal Judicial Response to Racism in the Early West." *Oregon Law Review* 63 (December 1984).

O'Brien, Claire. "'With One Mighty Pull': Interracial Town Boosting in Nicodemus, Kansas." *Great Plains Quarterly* 16 (spring 1996).

Ong, Paul. "An Ethnic Trade: The Chinese Laundries in Early California." *Journal of Ethnic Studies* 8 (winter 1981).

Quinn, Larry D. "'Chink Chink Chinaman': The Beginning of Nativism in Montana." *Pacific Northwest Quarterly* 58 (April 1987).

Rhoads, Edward J. M. "The Chinese in Texas." *Southwestern Historical Quarterly* 81 (July 1977).

Richard, K. Keith. "Unwelcomed Settlers: Blacks and Mulatto Oregon Pioneers, Part II." *Oregon Historical Quarterly* 84 (summer 1983).

Sheridan, Richard B. "From Slavery in Missouri to Freedom in Kansas: The Influx of Black Fugitives and Contrabands into Kansas, 1854–1865." *Kansas History* 12 (spring 1989).

Shoenberger, Dale T. "The Black Man in the American West." *Negro History Bulletin* 32 (March 1969).

Snorgrass, J. William. "The Black Press in the San Francisco Bay Area, 1856–1900." *California History* 60 (winter 1981–82).

Swartout, Robert R. Jr. "Kwantung to Big Sky: The Chinese in Montana, 1864–1900." *Montana, The Magazine of Western History* 38 (winter 1988).

Williams, Nudie E. "Black Newspapers and the Exodusters of 1879." *Kansas History* (winter 1985–1986).

Woods, Randall B. "Integration, Exclusion, or Segregation? The 'Color Line' in Kansas, 1878–1900." *Western Historical Quarterly* 14 (April 1983).

Wortman, Ron T. "Denver's Anti-Chinese Riot, 1880." *The Colorado Magazine* 42 (fall 1965).

Wright, Paul. "Population Patterns in Presidio County in 1880: Evidence from the Census." *Journal of Big Bend Studies* 7 (January 1995).

Wunder, John R. "Anti-Chinese Violence in the American West, 1850–1910." In *Law for the Elephant, Law for the Beaver: Essays in the History of the American West.* Edited by John R. McLaren, Hamar Foster, and Chet Orloff. Pasadena, Calif.: Ninth Judicial Circuit Historical Society, 1992.

———. "Law and Chinese in Frontier Montana." *Montana, The Magazine of Western History* 30 (1980).

Zhu, Liping. "How the Other Half Lived: Chinese Daily Life in Boise Basin Mining Camps." *Idaho Yesterdays* 38 (winter 1995).

Dissertations:

Chen, Chin-Yu. "San Francisco's Chinatown: A Socio-Economic and Cultural History, 1850–1882." Ph.D. Dissertation, University of Idaho, 1992.

Coleman, Ronald Gerald. "A History of Blacks in Utah, 1825–1910." Ph.D. Dissertation, University of Utah, 1980.

Hudson, Lynn M. "When 'Mammy' Became a Millionaire: Mary Ellen Pleasant, An African American Entrepreneur." Ph.D. Dissertation, Indiana University, 1996.

Lou, Raymond. "The Chinese American Community of Los Angeles, 1870–1900: A Case of Resistance, Organization, and Participation." Ph.D. Dissertation, University of California Irvine, 1982.

Xia, Yanwen. "The Sojourner Myth and Chinese Immigrants in the U.S." Ph.D. Dissertation, Bowling Green State University, 1993.

Xu, Shi. "The Image of the Chinese in the Rocky Mountain Region, 1855–1882." Ph.D. Dissertation, Brigham Young University, 1996.

Yu, Li-hua. "Chinese Immigrants in Idaho." Ph.D. Dissertation, Bowling Green State University, 1991.

Newspapers:

The Daily Ranchero, Brownsville, Texas, 1869.

Texas State Gazette, Austin, Texas, 1854.

Index